Welcome to our neighborhood...

w w w . n e l s o n d e s i g n g r o u p . c o m

"It's not just a home, it's a neighborhood." This primary philosophy has driven us since 1985, when we began sketching floor plans and developing custom blueprints for individual homebuyers. Today, Nelson Design Group, LLC incorporates unique designs, which complement each other and foster family values and traditional ideals. The result, an effective overall neighborhood design theme encouraging interaction not only between the family, but also between neighbors. At Nelson Design Group, our goal is to provide our clients with a design that perpetuates a constant feeling of pride. Each owner should step into their dream home each day knowing they made the best decision possible, not only with their home, but with their surroundings. Remember, with Nelson Design Group...It's not just a home, it's a neighborhood.

Best regards,

Michael E. Nelson
Founder & CEO

Nelson Design Group LLC

RESIDENTIAL PLANNERS - DESIGNERS

Call us today 800-590-2423 or visit
our website www.nelsondesigngroup.com
2200 Fowler Ave. - Suite D • Jonesboro, AR 72401

NDG304 - See page 87 to view floor plan

TABLE OF CONTENTS

Nelson Design Group LLC

RESIDENTIAL PLANNERS - DESIGNERS

www.nelsondesigngroup.com

NDG948

HOME PLANS

www.nelsondesigngroup.com

The NDG home features hearth rooms, privacy kids' nooks, computer centers, and home theater rooms blending yesterday's style with today's function and technology. Our custom-design philosophy has gained in popularity as an effective and creative solution for homebuyers seeking more than stock floor plans. **Our experienced staff of designers offers the qualities that an individual searching for a home desires - creativity and efficiency.** With our advanced technology, we can modify any of our plans to suit your needs - **saving time and guaranteeing customer satisfaction.** We are a nationally known residential design firm with plans published by Garlinghouse, Architectural Designs, Home Design Alternatives, BUILDER Magazine, Creative Homeowner, Home Planners, Better Homes and Gardens and others, as well as, numerous web sites including our own. National exposure enables NDG to maintain a leading edge in the design market. With Home Plans, Marketing, Tru-Cost Estimating, Land Planning and our new sister company NDG Commercial Division, Inc., we are able to provide for all your building needs. Our daily association with leading developers and builders keeps NDG at the forefront of the industry and attuned to the latest trends in design, construction methods, materials and products - for your benefit. Call our NDG Sales Specialists at 1-800-590-2423.

Charted Neighborhoods®

"Solutions for Master Planned Communities"
Planning - Home Design - Marketing

NDG314

Today, a public awakening now highly values its heritage of great neighborhoods. Updated interiors of the homes many of us grew up in are now incorporated into Neo-Traditional, or Traditional Neighborhood Design. Hence, the pursuit of the American Dream has taken an indirect path, away from suburban sprawl and back to a renewed appreciation of development patterns of our predecessors. Some of these planning and design principals date back to the late 1800's.

In more recent years, New Urbanism has caused a revival among historic towns, cities and villages, where the home-buying public wants more than just a place to sleep after work. A new appreciation for a richer social and civic life is integral to today's Master Planned Communities, in which families can get to know their neighbors by relaxing on spacious front porches and walking along tree covered streets and sidewalks.

To meet the rising demand of Traditional Neighborhood Designs, today's building professional is looking for a design firm that can be much more than just a vendor of stock plans. Until now, residential and commercial builders and developers have indicated that a true "total resource" for planning, design, cost-analysis and value-added marketing services, is almost unheard of. Most builders need a home plan source that essentially functions as their very own "in-house, complete source" for new home design and associated services. Nelson Design Group is a firm that concentrates on true personal service, and one that will modify plans as necessary, always delivering much more one on one attention that you deserve.

NDG304 - See page 87 to view floor plan

No longer will you need several firms to provide plans or modifications, and still be on your own to market the project afterwards. Regardless of your Company's size and volume, whether builder or developer, residential or commercial, we want to be your "personal design and promotional partner." We are ready to consult with you on individual plans or small in-fill projects, and yet we are large enough to work with you on the design of new large-scale Charted Neighborhood Communities. Quite simply, we do it all - always with a personal touch and at a reasonable fee.

Because builders and developers across the country already rely on us to provide their plans and marketing resources, we cater daily to a diverse marketplace with a broad mix of consumers, real estate professionals and home builders. We know what buyers want, how builders "build" and how to design and market homes that sell quickly. Each Nelson Design Group plan offers stunning elevations and fresh interior floor plans with unique features such as kid's nooks, hearth rooms, home theater or media rooms and grilling porches to attract homeowner interests and promote a carefree lifestyle. Our designs are supported with our wide array of economically customized marketing materials to promote your project during construction, and then facilitate a quick sale – often at premium appraisal values.

In the following pages, you will find individual designs and numerous groups of plans –our collections– such as our new Heritage, Midtown Village, Midtown Estate, Midtown Place, and Aronson Mediterranean Collections. Our designs have complementary themes that work together to build a single home, a neighborhood, or a full-scale development. There is certainly something you can immediately incorporate into your building program.

NDG304
See page 87 to view floor plan

When online, point your browser to our comprehensive website, www.nelsondesigngroup.com. Our site features a handy "search" option where you can select from hundreds of plans to simplify locating designs that accommodate your lot dimensions and preferred architectural style. Give us a call or send us an e-mail. Above all, please let us know if you have any questions or special requirements. We are always interested in hearing about your projects and how we might serve you now – and in the future.

As we say, "Welcome to our Neighborhood..." On behalf of Michael E. Nelson and our entire staff of friendly designers, marketing specialists, cost-analysts and customer service team, we are pleased to introduce Nelson Design Group, LLC, America's fastest growing residential design, planning, and marketing firm, as well as NDG Commercial Division, Inc., President Matt Silas, Architect.

Midtown Estate Collection - page 18

CHARTED NEIGHBORHOODS®

A "Charted Neighborhood" is Nelson Design Group's approach for design "plus" marketing services making your job easier when developing "Master Planned Communities." The neighborhoods are created to save time and provide consistency with a design theme that is complementary. As the name implies, a *Charted Neighborhood® represents a distinctive new direction and concept in residential design with marketing* – an approach that is unique to Nelson Design Group. Call 1-800-590-2423 for more details.

Renaissance – A French Country Neighborhood

545 Calais Drive

Heritage Collection™

947 Ambrose Boulevard

Midtown Estate Collection™

918 Summer Avenue

The Providian™ Collection

645 Providian Place

Architectural Stock Plans™ – A Collection of Commercial Designs

NDG-C109

The Florida Collection™

561 The Clarion

The Waterfront™ Collection

833 Waterfront Cove

The River Bend™ Collection

415 Creek Side

Historical™ Collection

785 Madison Avenue

The Burlington™ Collection

638 Burlington Cove

Village at Windstone™

308 Windstone Place

Village at Windstone II™

337 Windstone Place

Village at Windstone III™

391 Windstone Place

The Urban™ Collection

402 Urban Lane

Jim Barna Log Systems

1007 The Baxter

The Multi-Family Collection™

661 Heather Ridge

The Olde Towne Collection™

819 Mulberry Lane

Sage Meadows™ Collection

277 Sage Meadows

The Village at Wellington™

270 Wellington Lane

Stone™ Village

828 Woodland Drive

The Cross Creek™ Collection

303 Cross Creek

Midtown Village™ Collection

925 Park Street

Arts&Crafts™ collection – "A step back in time"

586 Ivy

Aronson Mediterranean™ Collection

1525 Ocean Drive

Midtown Place™ – The place where memories begin...

988 Georgia Avenue

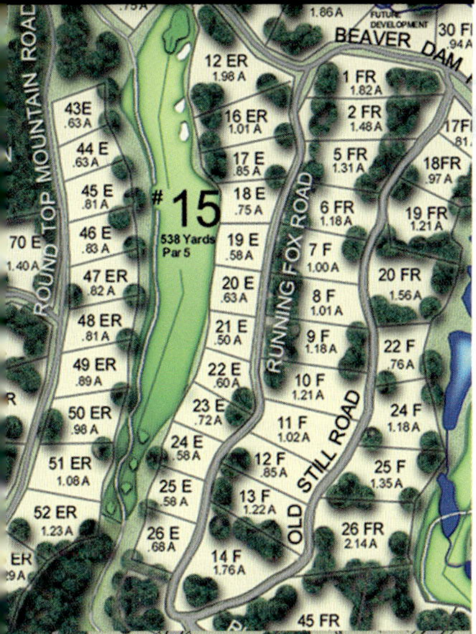

LAND PLANNING

www.nelsondesigngroup.com

Nelson Design Group works with builders and developers during the conceptualization phase of land use planning. We provide valuable expertise from site selection to proper land use. We can recommend the appropriate lot sizes to maximize the best use for the land and assist in creating effective neighborhoods. **Our services during these early development stages help builders avoid costly revisions in design and engineering.** Call our NDG Sales Specialists for details - 1-800-590-2423.

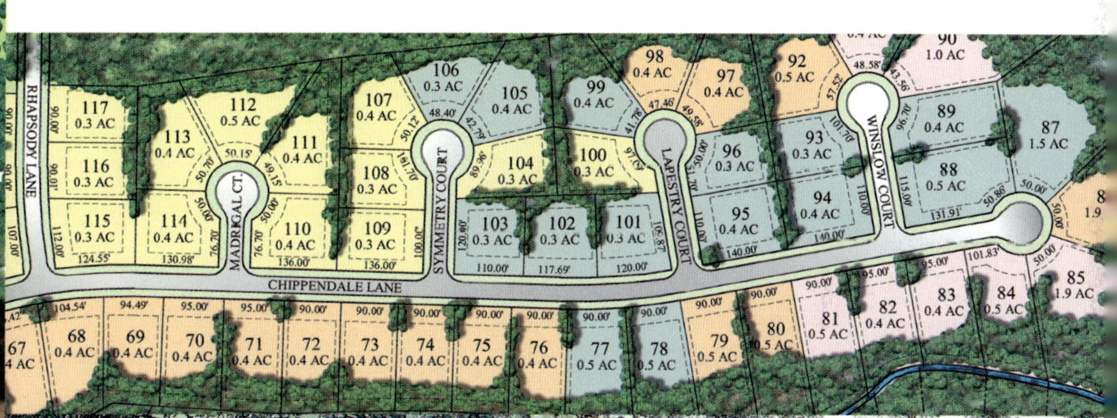

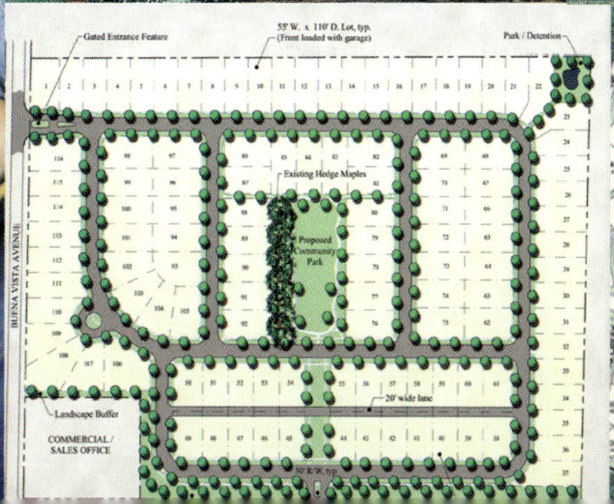

TRU-COST ESTIMATING

www.nelsondesigngroup.com

Tru-Cost ESTIMATING

The Industry's New Standard for Home Plan Estimating

Tru-Cost Estimating is a valuable tool for use in the planning and construction of your new home. Tru-Cost Estimates are available for each of NDG's stock plans as well as any modified NDG plan or custom plan. We provide a complete estimate, similar to a bid, that will act as a checklist for all items and products you will need to select or coordinate during your building process. Tru-Cost will provide you a direct comparison to track your costs and help you stay within budget.

Also available - Tru-Cost Software has options that allow you to customize your estimate, to include labor rates and material prices for your area and can be imported into your Tru-Cost Software. The key to a successful project is to have a realistic budget, Tru-Cost is the solution. Call our NDG Sales Specialists for details - 1-800-590-2423.

Try Tru-Cost today to see why professional estimators praise our product.

See page 96 for ordering information

Bid Overview

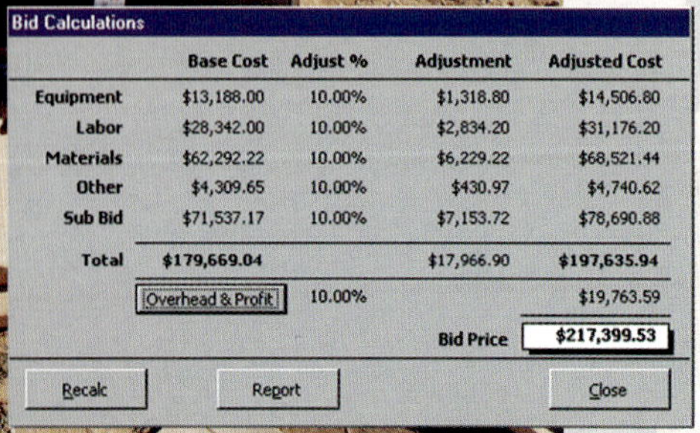

Bid Calculations

	Base Cost	Adjust %	Adjustment	Adjusted Cost
Equipment	$13,188.00	10.00%	$1,318.80	$14,506.80
Labor	$28,342.00	10.00%	$2,834.20	$31,176.20
Materials	$62,292.22	10.00%	$6,229.22	$68,521.44
Other	$4,309.65	10.00%	$430.97	$4,740.62
Sub Bid	$71,537.17	10.00%	$7,153.72	$78,690.88
Total	$179,669.04		$17,966.90	$197,635.94
	Overhead & Profit	10.00%		$19,763.59
			Bid Price	$217,399.53

Recalc Report Close

Itemized Listing

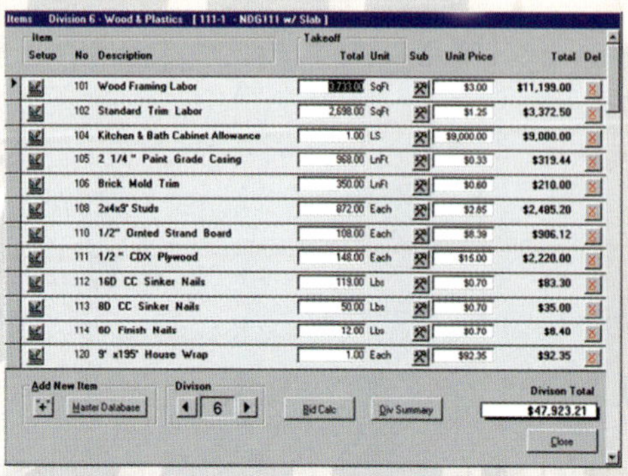

Items Division 6 - Wood & Plastics [111-1 - NDG111 w/ Slab]

Item Setup	No	Description	Takeoff Total	Unit	Sub	Unit Price	Total	Del
	101	Wood Framing Labor	3,733.00	SqFt		$3.00	$11,199.00	
	102	Standard Trim Labor	2,698.00	SqFt		$1.25	$3,372.50	
	104	Kitchen & Bath Cabinet Allowance	1.00	LS		$9,000.00	$9,000.00	
	105	2 1/4" Paint Grade Casing	968.00	LnFt		$0.33	$319.44	
	106	Brick Mold Trim	350.00	LnFt		$0.60	$210.00	
	108	2x4x9' Studs	872.00	Each		$2.85	$2,485.20	
	110	1/2" Ornted Strand Board	108.00	Each		$8.39	$906.12	
	111	1/2" CDX Plywood	148.00	Each		$15.00	$2,220.00	
	112	16D CC Sinker Nails	119.00	Lbs		$0.70	$83.30	
	113	8D CC Sinker Nails	50.00	Lbs		$0.70	$35.00	
	114	6D Finish Nails	12.00	Lbs		$0.70	$8.40	
	120	9' x195' House Wrap	1.00	Each		$92.35	$92.35	

Add New Item: Master Database; Divison: 6; Bid Calc; Div Summary; Divison Total: $47,923.21; Close

Ledger Entry Form

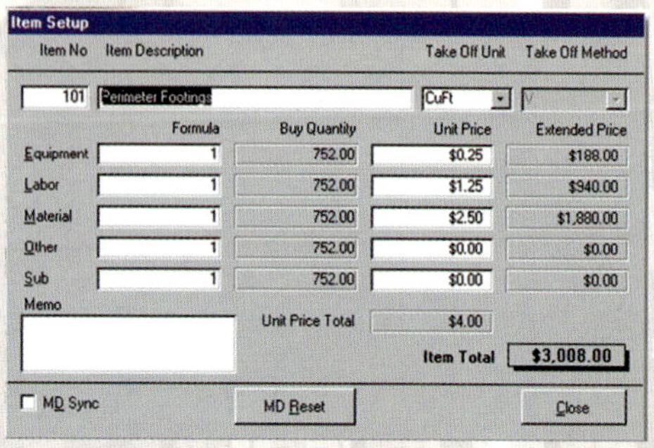

Item Setup

Item No: 101 | Item Description: Perimeter Footings | Take Off Unit: CuFt | Take Off Method: V

	Formula	Buy Quantity	Unit Price	Extended Price
Equipment	1	752.00	$0.25	$188.00
Labor	1	752.00	$1.25	$940.00
Material	1	752.00	$2.50	$1,880.00
Other	1	752.00	$0.00	$0.00
Sub	1	752.00	$0.00	$0.00

Memo

Unit Price Total: $4.00

Item Total: $3,008.00

MD Sync MD Reset Close

MARKETING

www.nelsondesigngroup.com

Nelson Design Group offers marketing materials for each of our home plans and can easily customize them to fit your specific needs. A developer, whether large or small, can have cost effective marketing tools on the property while under construction and framed in the office, or available for handouts. Utilizing Nelson Design Group's advertising tools and services will save you time and money in developing your effective marketing strategy.

Call our NDG Sales Specialists for details - 1-800-590-2423.

Testimonials

I bought one of the yard signs and placed it on my lot. I had not begun any construction at this point and within one week - the house sold!

Tommy Lovrien,
TL Construction, LLC

The new yard signs with feature sheet holder are outstanding. I had a call from a prospective customer the first day the sign went up!

Gregg Black,
GHB Construction and Development Co., Inc.

Yard Signs

Feature Sheet Holder

Product Portfolios

Feature Sheets

Builder Identity Kit

Framed & Matted Prints

Brochures & Programs

Watercolor Architectural Renderings

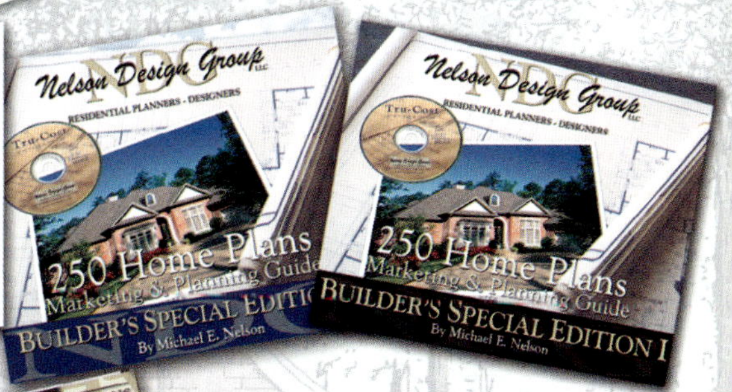

Home Plan Books

COMMERCIAL STOCK PLANS

see these commercial plans and many more at www.nelsondesigngroup.com

Matt Silas, AIA utilizes experience of over twelve years in the architectural industry. He has produced and provided complete architectural services on a variety of design project types. Professional Affiliations include AIA - Member of the American Institute of Architects and NCARB - Member of the National Council of Architectural Registration Board.

"Our mission is to provide design services which exceed our client's expectations." Matt Silas, AIA

NDG-C111

Toll Free 866-932-5910

Available Commercial Concept Stock Plan Types

Offices, Retail, Maintenance, Cinema, Multi-Family, Food Service, Religious, Medical, Industrial, Plus Many More

NDG Commercial Division INC.
ARCHITECTURE & PLANNING

NDG-C141

Matt Silas, AIA

NDG-C143

NDG-C104

NDG-C115

NDG-C142

NDG-C106

NDG-C103

NDG Commercial Division, Inc. Concept Stock Plans

available at

www.nelsondesigngroup.com

NDG-C145

NDG-C144

NDG-C146

NDG Commercial Division, Inc. Concept Stock Plans

available at

www.nelsondesigngroup.com

NDG-C112

NDG-C137

NDG-C123

NDG Commercial Division, Inc. Commercial Concept Stock Plans are designs generated to provide an Owner or Developer with an advanced placement in the project development saving time and money as a result of a shorter design process. Commercial Concept Stock Plans may be purchased by an Owner or Developer and used by other design professionals for construction document development and adaptation to a particular site. **Commercial Concept Stock Plans will include the following drawings:**

- Cover Sheet / Rendering
- Floor Plan(s)
- Exterior Elevations
- Building Sections
- Wall Sections
- Room Finish, Door and Window Schedules
- Interior Elevations, Enlarged Plans and / or Details
- Roof Plan

Structural, Mechanical, Plumbing and Electrical drawings can be provided under additional services and fees.

Additional Architectural and Engineering professionals are required to convert the conceptual drawings into the necessary construction documents conforming to respective codes where the project is to be located. As an Owner or Developer, you have the option of hiring local Architects for construction document development or NDG Commercial Division, Inc. can provide complete, sealed construction documents as an additional architectural service for all Commercial Concept Stock Plans in states where licensed. Please call **Matt Silas, AIA**, President of NDG Commercial Division, Inc. at 1-866-932-5910 for complete details.

NDG
Commercial Division INC.
ARCHITECTURE & PLANNING

Browse and purchase online

www.nelsondesigngroup.com

"Your Home Plan Source & More"

When online, point your browser to our comprehensive website, nelsondesigngroup.com. Our site features a handy "search" option where you can select from hundreds of plans to simplify locating designs that accommodate your lot dimensions and preferred architectural style. Give us a call or send us an e-mail. Above all, please let us know if you have any questions or special requirements. We are always interested in hearing about your projects and how we might serve you now – and in the future.

- Home Plans
- Land Planning
- Stock Landscape Plans
- Tru-Cost Estimating
- Commercial Stock Plans™
- Marketing
- Interior Solutions

NDG Nelson Design Group LLC

RESIDENTIAL PLANNERS - DESIGNERS

1-800-590-2423

www.nelsondesigngroup.com

NDG Featured Collection 1st Release 2005

Heritage™ NDG SINCE • 1985 COLLECTION

17 Featuring NDG Plans

The Heritage Collection represents seventeen homes ranging in square footage of 2400 to 3200 with unique 'theater balconies.'

Main Floor

Upper Floor

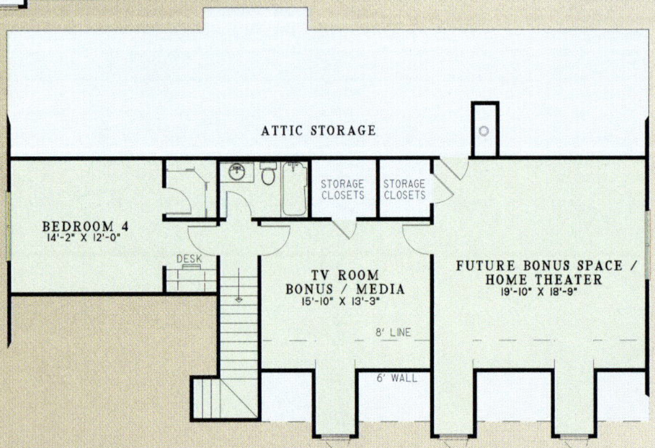

NDG948

NDG957

NDG953

953 Ambrose Boulevard

Width: 60' 0"
Depth: 77' 6"
Main Floor: 2,129 sq. ft.
Upper Floor: 316 sq. ft.
Total Living: 2,445 sq. ft.*
***Bonus:** 758 sq. ft
Main Ceiling: 9 ft.
Upper Ceiling: 8 ft.

Bedrooms: 4
Baths: 3 1/2
Foundation: Crawl, Slab, Optional Basement, Optional Daylight Basement
Plan Options: page 93

Price Tier: C

To view all the plans in this collection visit www.nelsondesigngroup.com

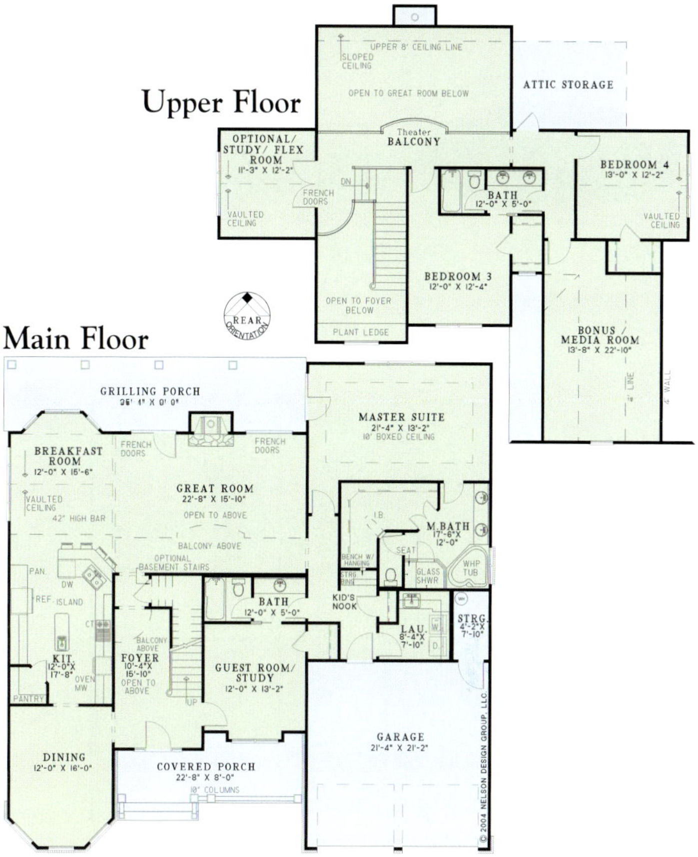

950 Ambrose Boulevard

Width: 57' 4"
Depth: 55' 10"
Main Floor: 2,142 sq. ft.
Upper Floor: 673 sq. ft.
Total Living: 2,815 sq. ft.*
*Bonus: 455 sq. ft.
Main Ceiling: 9 ft.
Upper Ceiling: 8 ft.

Bedrooms: 4
Baths: 3
Foundation: Crawl, Slab, Optional Basement, Optional Daylight Basement
Plan Options: page 93

Price Tier: D

Similar plans can be viewed and ordered at www.nelsondesigngroup.com

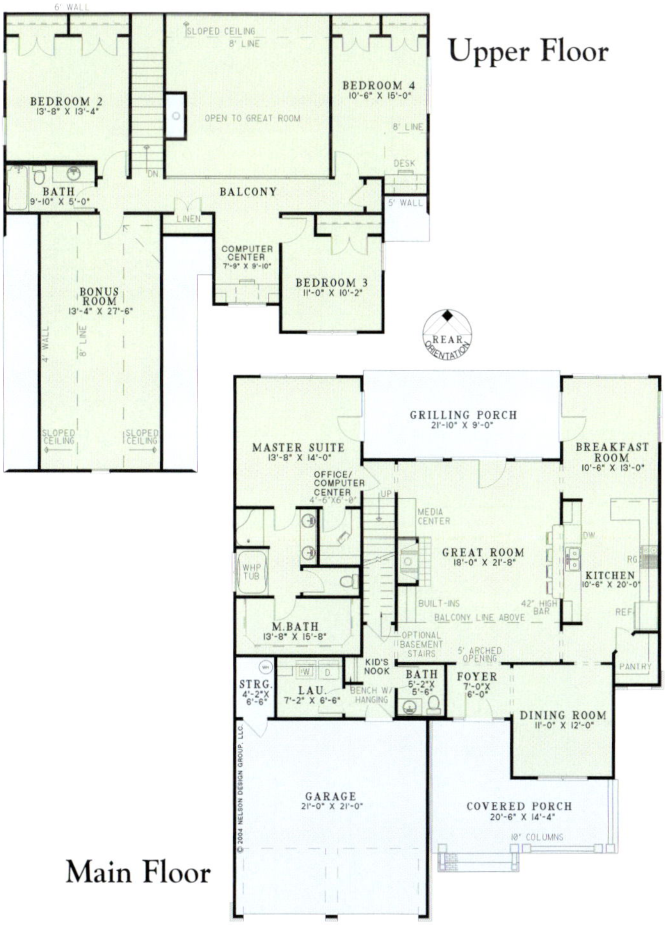

844 Ambrose Boulevard

Width: 47' 4"
Depth: 58' 8"
Main Floor: 1,595 sq. ft.
Upper Floor: 875 sq. ft.
Total Living: 2,470 sq. ft.*
*Bonus: 389 sq. ft.
Main Ceiling: 9 ft.
Upper Ceiling: 8 ft.

Bedrooms: 4
Baths: 2 1/2
Foundation: Crawl, Slab, Optional Basement, Optional Daylight Basement
Plan Options: page 93

Price Tier: C

Upper Floor

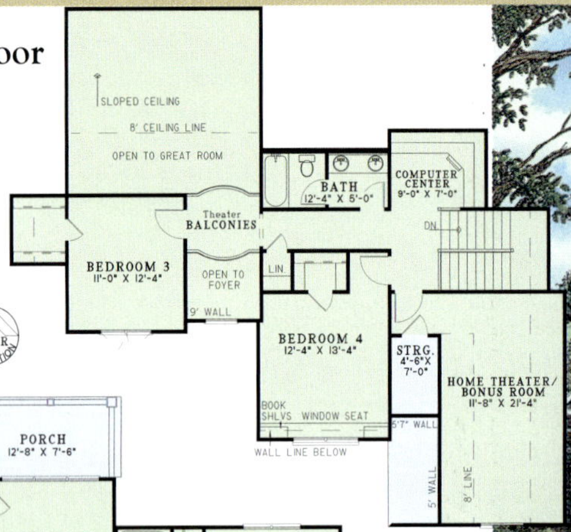

NDG Featured Collection 1st Release 2005
Heritage NDG SINCE 1985
COLLECTION

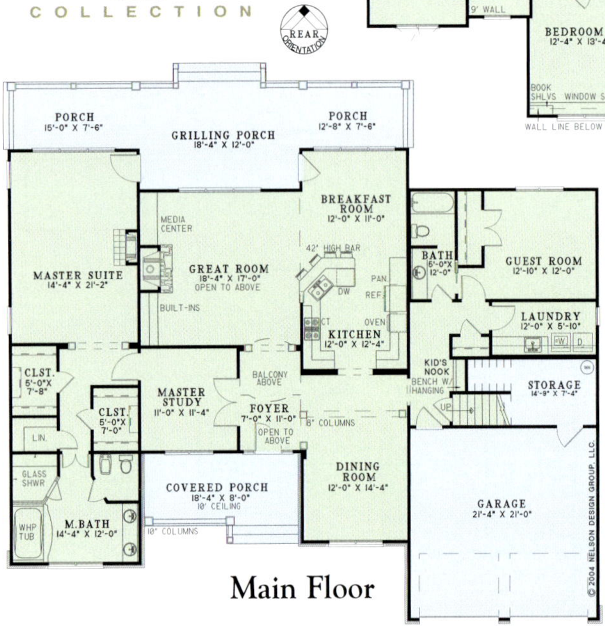

Main Floor

948 Ambrose Boulevard

Width: 67' 8"
Depth: 60' 0"
Main Floor: 2,266 sq. ft.
Upper Floor: 686 sq. ft.
Total Living: 2,952 sq. ft.*
*Bonus: 318 sq. ft
Main Ceiling: 9 ft.
Upper Ceiling: 8 ft.

Bedrooms: 4
Baths: 3
Foundation: Crawl, Slab, Optional Basement, Optional Daylight Basement
Plan Options: page 93

Price Tier: D

To order call toll free 1-800-590-2423

Main Floor

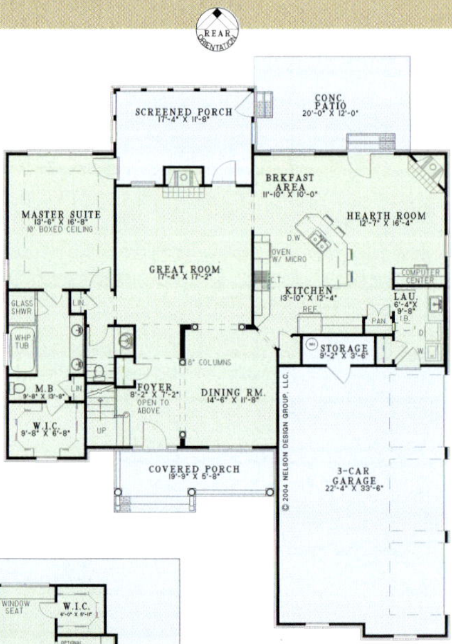

NDG Featured Collection 1st Release 2005
Heritage NDG SINCE 1985
COLLECTION

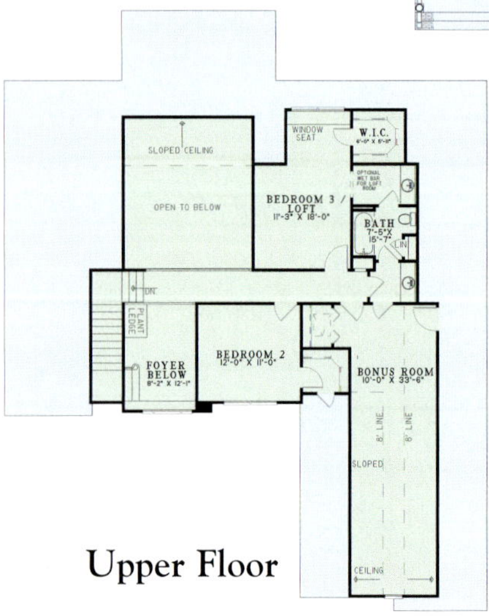

Upper Floor

954 Ambrose Boulevard

Width: 56' 8"
Depth: 68' 8"
Main Floor: 1,770 sq. ft.
Upper Floor: 584 sq. ft.
Total Living: 2,354 sq. ft.*
*Bonus: 385 sq. ft
Main Ceiling: 9 ft.
Upper Ceiling: 8 ft.

Bedrooms: 3
Baths: 2 1/2
Foundation: Crawl, Slab, Optional Basement, Optional Daylight Basement
Plan Options: page 93

Price Tier: C

Similar plans can be viewed and ordered at www.nelsondesigngroup.com

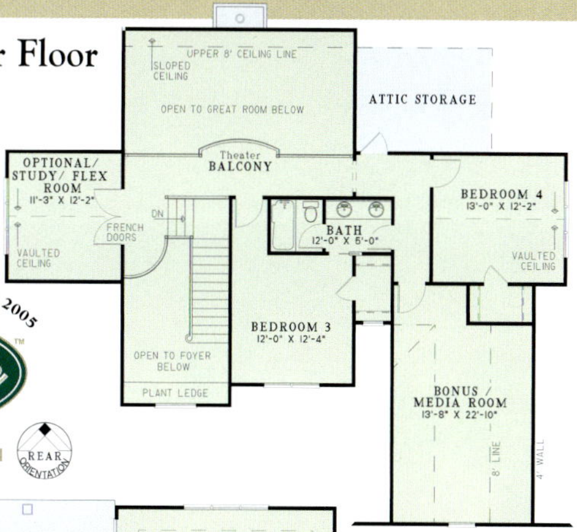

NDG Featured Collection 1st Release 2005
Heritage NDG SINCE 1985
COLLECTION
REAR ORIENTATION

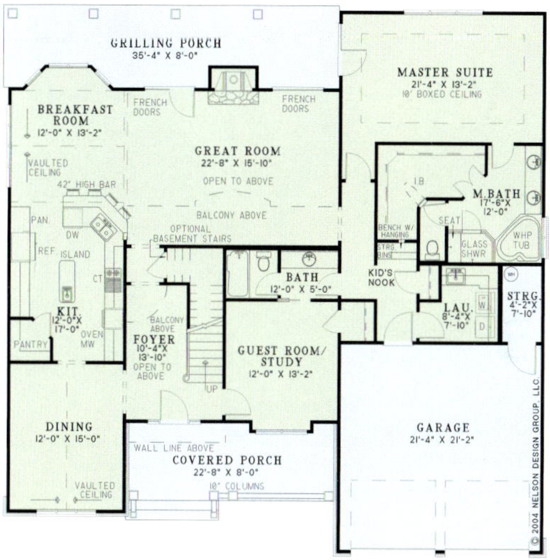

947 Ambrose Boulevard

Width: 57' 4"
Depth: 55' 10"
Main Floor: 2,084 sq. ft.
Upper Floor: 671 sq. ft.
Total Living: 2,755 sq. ft.*
***Bonus:** 454 sq. ft
Main Ceiling: 9 ft.
Upper Ceiling: 8 ft.

Bedrooms: 4
Baths: 3
Foundation: Crawl, Slab, Optional Basement, Optional Daylight Basement
Plan Options: page 93

Price Tier: D

Similar plans can be viewed and ordered at www.nelsondesigngroup.com

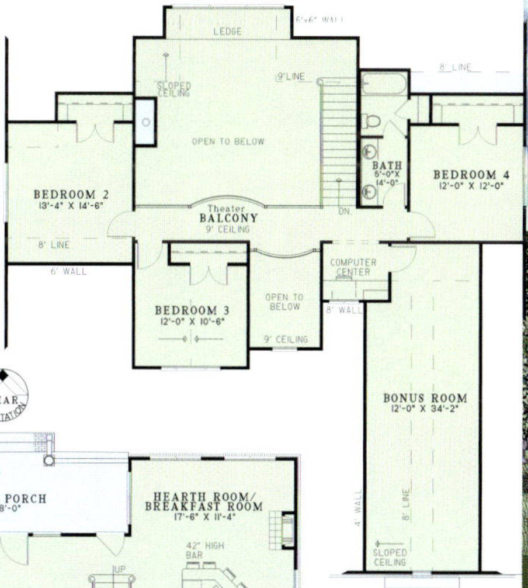

NDG Featured Collection 1st Release 2005
Heritage NDG SINCE 1985
COLLECTION
REAR ORIENTATION

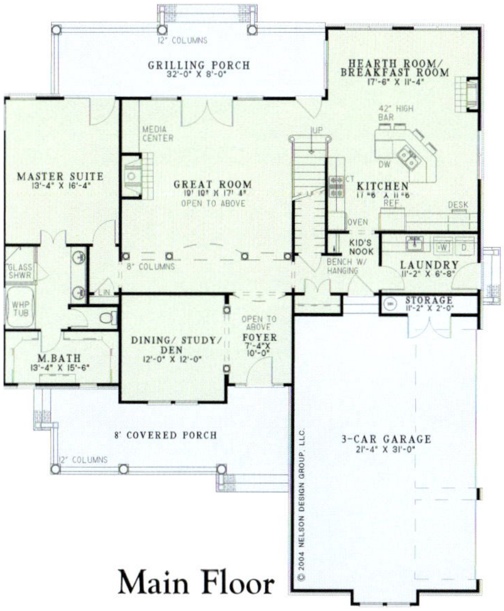

949 Ambrose Boulevard

Width: 55' 10"
Depth: 65' 8"
Main Floor: 1,793 sq. ft.
Upper Floor: 858 sq. ft.
Total Living: 2,651 sq. ft.*
***Bonus:** 418 sq. ft
Main Ceiling: 9 ft.
Upper Ceiling: 8 ft.

Bedrooms: 4
Baths: 2
Foundation: Crawl, Slab, Optional Basement, Optional Daylight Basement
Plan Options: page 93

Price Tier: D

Midtown ESTATE COLLECTION™

6 Featuring NDG Plans

Reminiscent of the Craftsman style era, these six two-story designs have porte cocheres and side-load garages, grilling porches, elegant finials and cupolas to detail the high pitched roof lines and living spaces ranging from 2,500 to 4,000 square feet.

NDG920

NDG919

NDG922

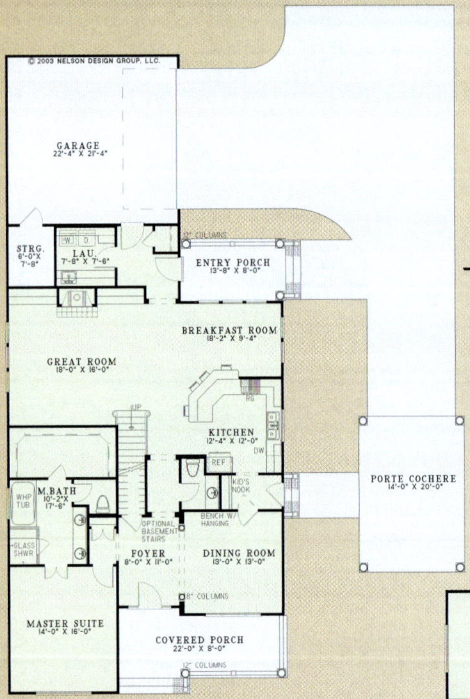

Main Floor

Upper Floor

NDG921

921 Summer Avenue

Width: 60' 8"
Depth: 82' 0"
Main Floor: 1,796 sq. ft.
Upper Floor: 1,194 sq. ft.
Total Living: 2,990 sq. ft.*
***Bonus:** 667 sq. ft.
Main Ceiling: 9 ft.
Upper Ceiling: 8 ft.

Bedrooms: 4
Baths: 3 1/2
Foundation: Crawl, Slab, Optional Basement, Optional Daylight Basement
Plan Options: page 93

Price Tier: D

Midtown Village COLLECTION™

15 Featuring NDG Plans

These fifteen home designs have style reflective of the arts and crafts era with unique porte cocheres leading to side-loading garages. A true country style is achieved by many exterior details including grilling porches. With living spaces ranging from 1,800 to 2,600 square feet, the interiors have all of the amenities families demand.

NDG925

NDG924

NDG934

NDG933

933 Park Street

Width: 62' 0"
Depth: 87' 6"
Total Living: 1,966 sq. ft.
Main Ceiling: 9 ft.
Bedrooms: 3
Baths: 2

Foundation: Crawl, Slab, Optional Basement, Optional Daylight Basement
Plan Options: page 93

Price Tier: B

Midtown Place™

The place where memories begin...

12 Premiering NDG Plans

NDG988

988 Georgia Avenue

Width: 116' 0"
Depth: 68' 6"
Home 1-
Main Floor: 1,360 sq. ft.
Upper Floor: 1,156 sq. ft.
Total Living: 2,516 sq. ft.*
Combined Living: 5,032 sq.ft.
Main Ceiling: 9 ft.
Upper Ceiling: 8 ft.

Bedrooms: 5
Baths: 3 **Half Baths:** 1
Foundation: Crawl, Slab, Optional Basement Optional Daylight Basement
Plan Options: page 93

Price Tier: G

These outstanding designs are reminiscent of years-gone-by. Family-oriented amenities including kid's nooks and computer centers will cater to the largest of families while timeless porte cocheres leading to private garages add to the neighborly appeal. Spacious bedrooms and dining areas with nearby grilling porches allow for plenty of gathering space.

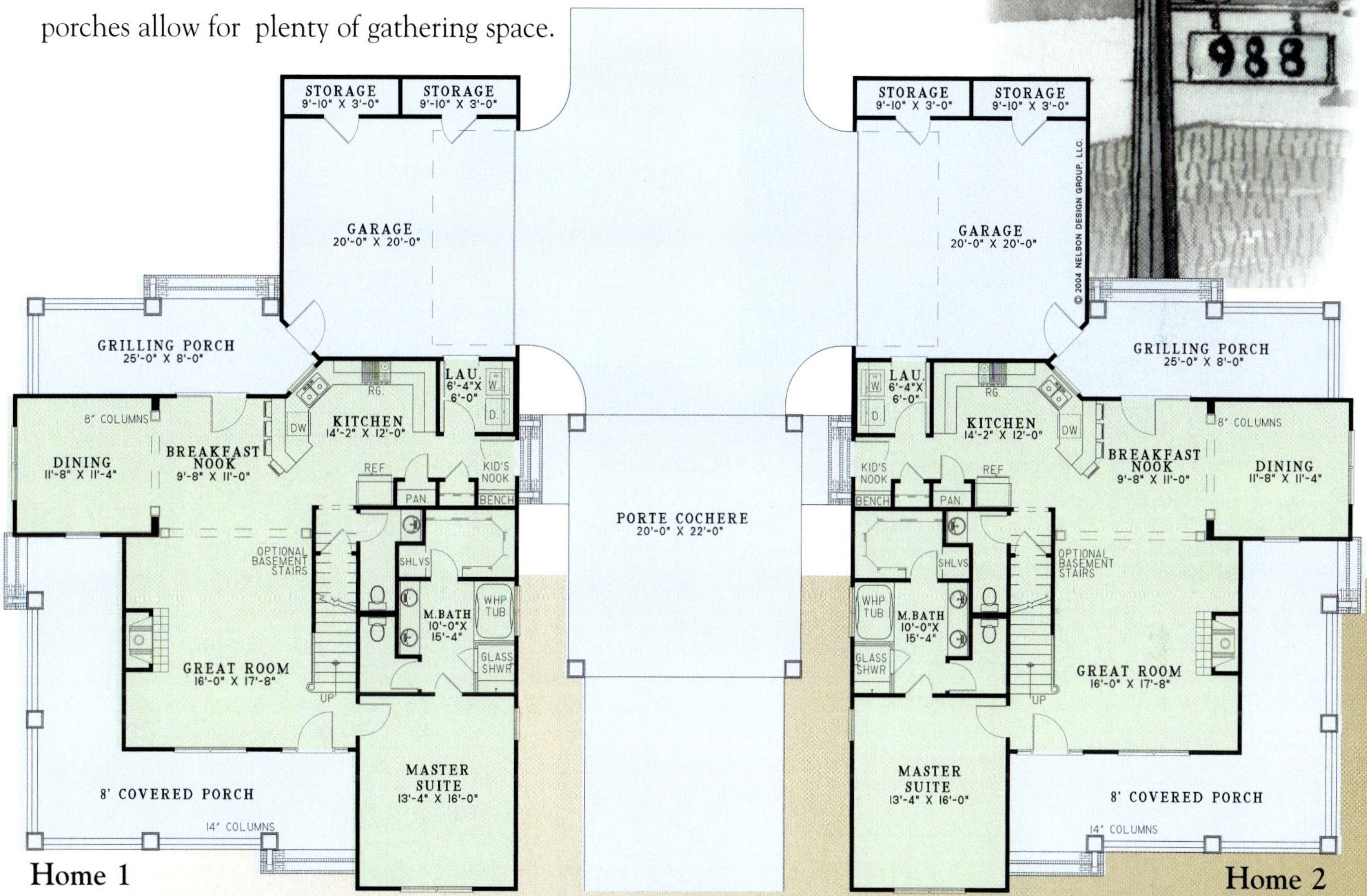

Home 1

Home 2

Main Floor

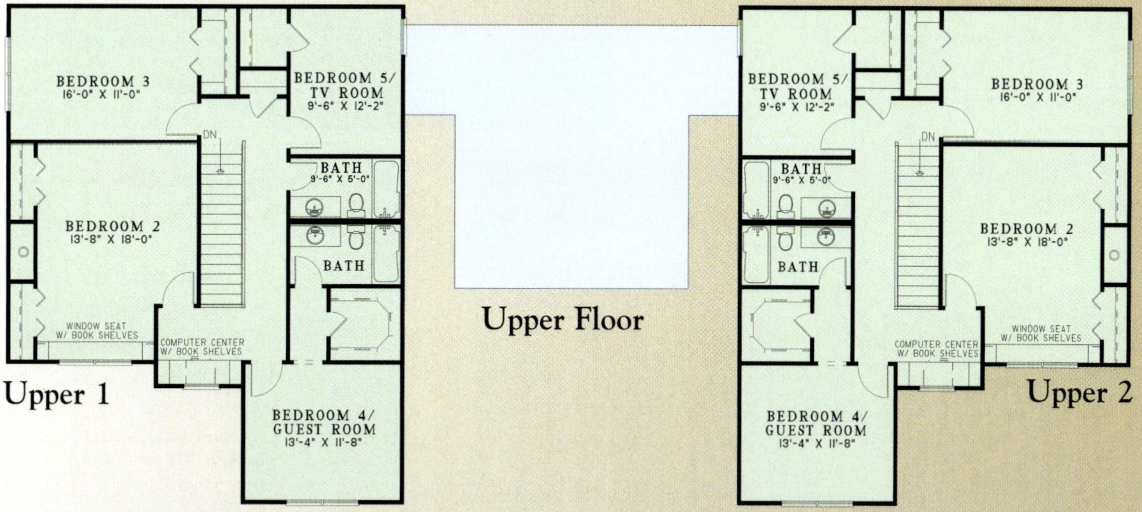

Upper Floor

Upper 1

Upper 2

Arts&Crafts™ collection

"A step back in time"

14 Featuring NDG Plans

Timeless designs celebrating the most functional use of space and craftsmanship. These fourteen narrow-lot home plans have living spaces of 1,200 to 2,300 square feet.

NDG586

NDG630

NDG596

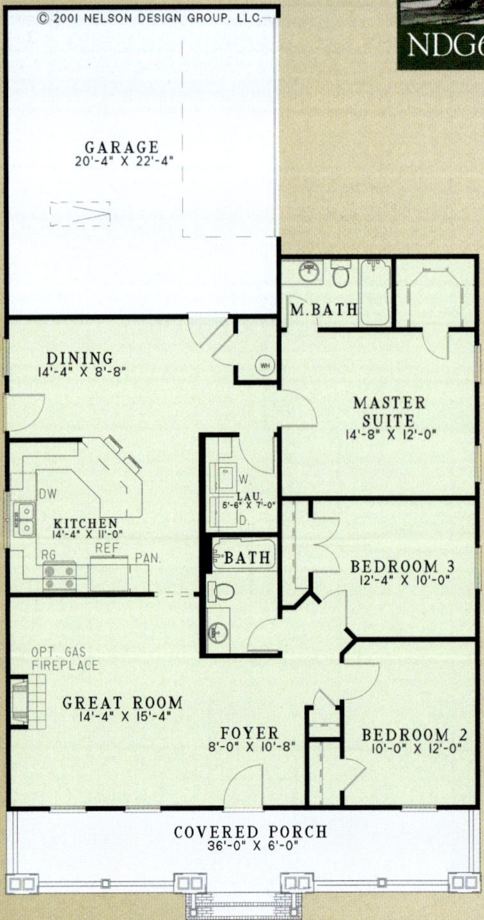

NDG625

625 Sycamore

Width: 36' 0"
Depth: 65' 0"
Total Living: 1,374 sq. ft.
Main Ceiling: 9 ft.
Bedrooms: 3
Baths: 2

Foundation: Crawl, Slab, Optional Basement, Optional Daylight Basement
Plan Options: page 93

Price Tier: A

To view all the plans in these collections visit www.nelsondesigngroup.com

THE PROVIDIAN™ COLLECTION

5 Featuring NDG Plans

The Providian Collection includes five economical home designs featuring living spaces of 1,300 to 1,800 square feet. Great starter homes - a Builder's dream!

NDG642

NDG643

NDG641

NDG645

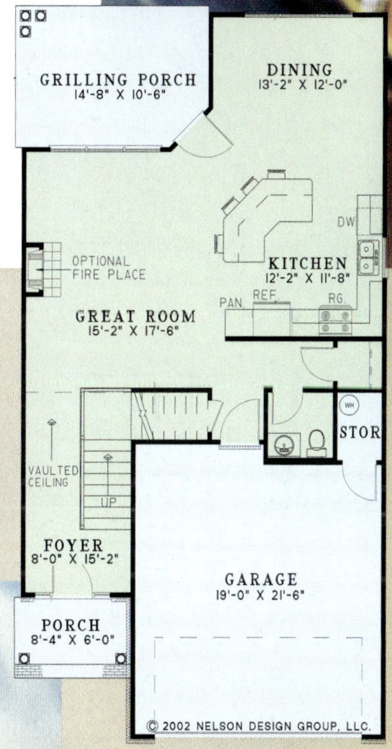

Main Floor

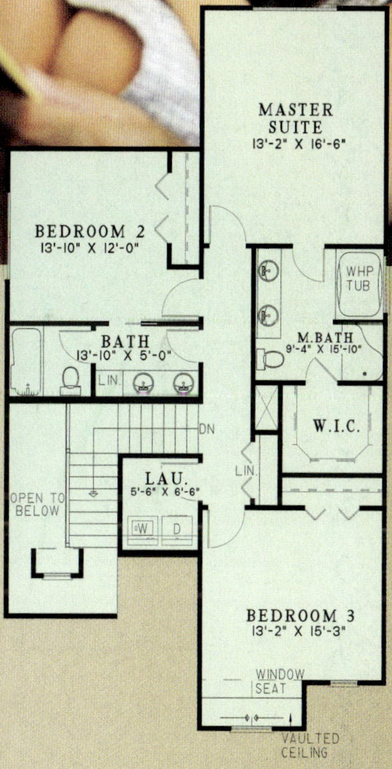

Upper Floor

645 Providian Place

Width: 28' 0"
Depth: 53' 10"
Main Floor: 851 sq. ft.
Upper Floor: 990 sq. ft.
Total Living: 1,841 sq. ft.
Main Ceiling: 9 ft.
Upper Ceiling: 8 ft.

Bedrooms: 3
Baths: 2 1/2
Foundation: Crawl, Slab, Optional Basement, Optional Daylight Basement
Plan Options: page 93

Price Tier: B

Village at WINDSTONE™

33 Featuring NDG Plans

With over 33 homes, these Traditional Neighborhood Designs are historically inspired - like Grandmother's home. **Village at Windstone**, **Windstone II,** and **Windstone III** homes range between 1,600 to 3,200 square feet providing ample amenities for the family.

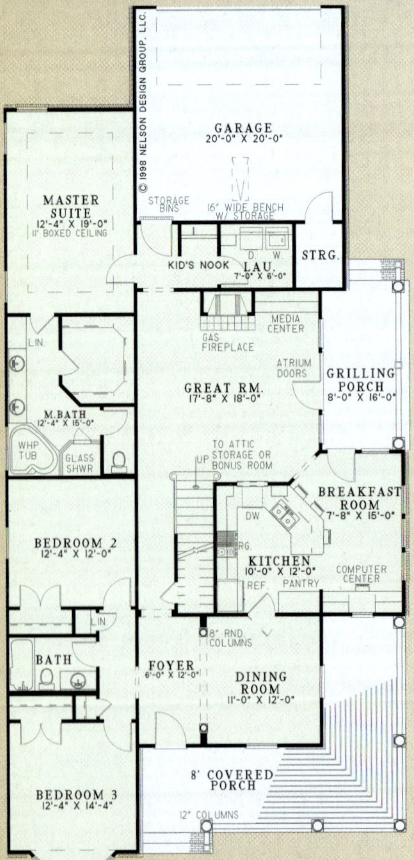

Main Floor

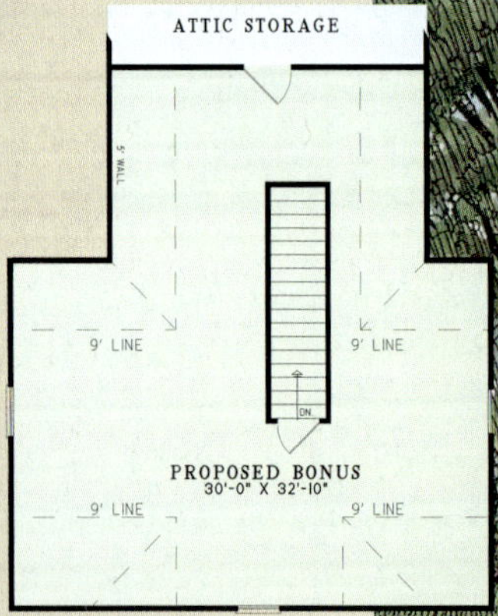

Bonus Floor

355 Windstone Place

Width: 39' 0"
Depth: 82' 4"
Total Living: 1,927 sq. ft.*
*** Bonus:** 909 sq. ft.
Main Ceiling: 10 ft.
Bonus Ceiling: 9 ft.

Bedrooms: 3
Baths: 2
Foundation: Crawl, Slab, Basement, Daylight Basement
Plan Options: page 93

Price Tier: B

To view all the plans in these collections visit www.nelsondesigngroup.com

THE URBAN™ COLLECTION

8 Featuring NDG Plans

Eight smaller Traditional Neighborhood Designs with rear-loading garages ranging from 1,100 to 1,600 square feet. The ultimate narrow lot designs for Master-planned developments.

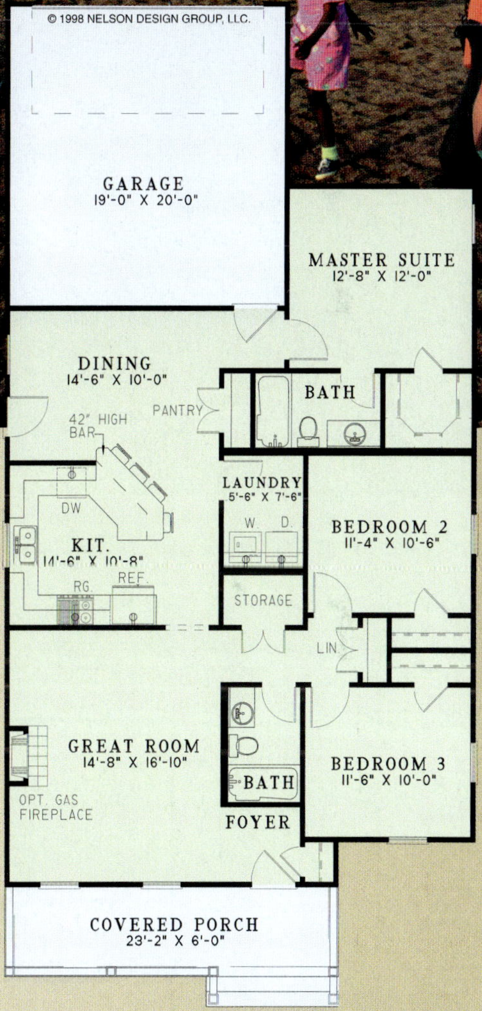

NDG794

NDG397

NDG399

NDG400

400 Urban Lane

Width: 32' 8"
Depth: 64' 10"
Total Living: 1,342 sq. ft.
Main Ceiling: 9 ft.
Bedrooms: 3
Baths: 2

Foundation: Crawl, Slab, Optional Basement, Optional Daylight Basement
Plan Options: page 93

Price Tier: A

THE Cross Creek™ COLLECTION

6 Featuring NDG Plans

These six traditional narrow lot designs range from 1,400 to just under 1,800 square feet. Simple yet refined - enjoying a bit of European flavor.

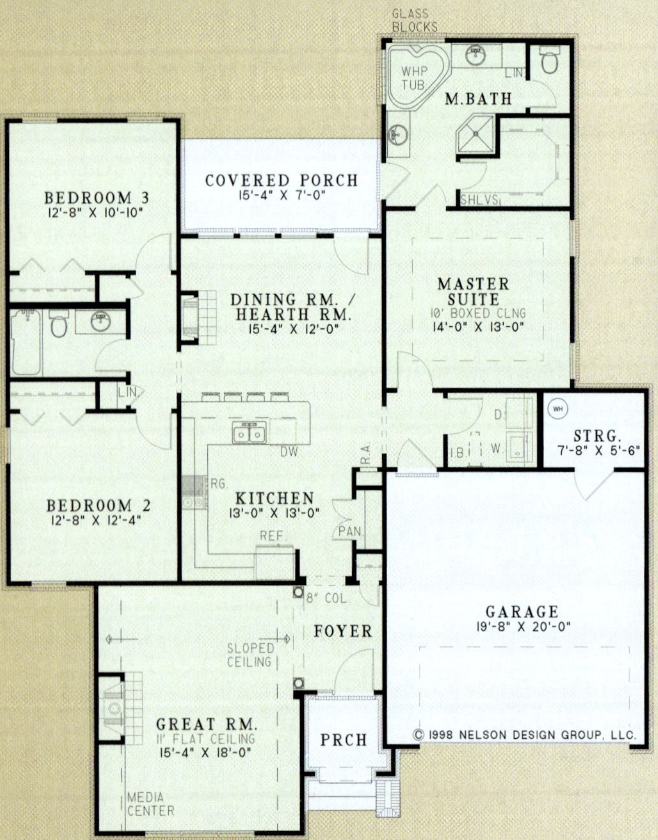

301 Cross Creek

Width: 49' 0"
Depth: 58' 6"
Total Living: 1,654 sq. ft.
Main Ceiling: 9 ft.
Bedrooms: 3
Baths: 2

Foundation: Crawl, Slab, Basement, Daylight Basement
Plan Options: page 93

Price Tier: B

To view all the plans in these collections visit www.nelsondesigngroup.com

The Village at Wellington™

14 Featuring NDG Plans

This collection of 14 charming home plans has square footages ranging from 1,000 to 1,600. Great for narrow lots and Traditional Neighborhood communities.

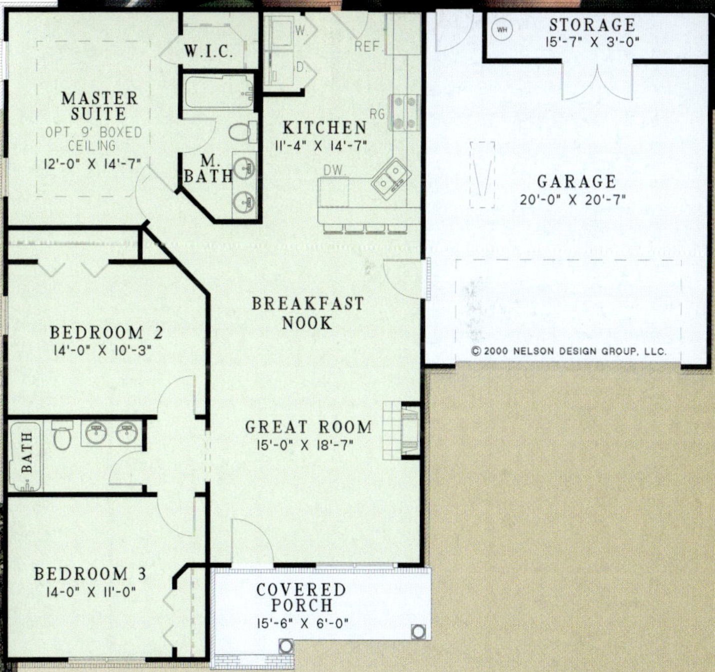

525 Wellington Lane

Width: 50' 4"
Depth: 45' 0"
Total Living: 1,250 sq. ft.
Main Ceiling: 8 ft.
Bedrooms: 3
Baths: 2

Foundation: Crawl, Slab, Optional Basement, Optional Daylight Basement
Plan Options: page 93

Price Tier: A

Sage Meadows™ COLLECTION

12 Featuring NDG Plans

French Country designs featuring 12 plans with living spaces of 1,200 to 1,600 square feet. These rear oriented narrow lot plans are perfect for lake views and golf course communities.

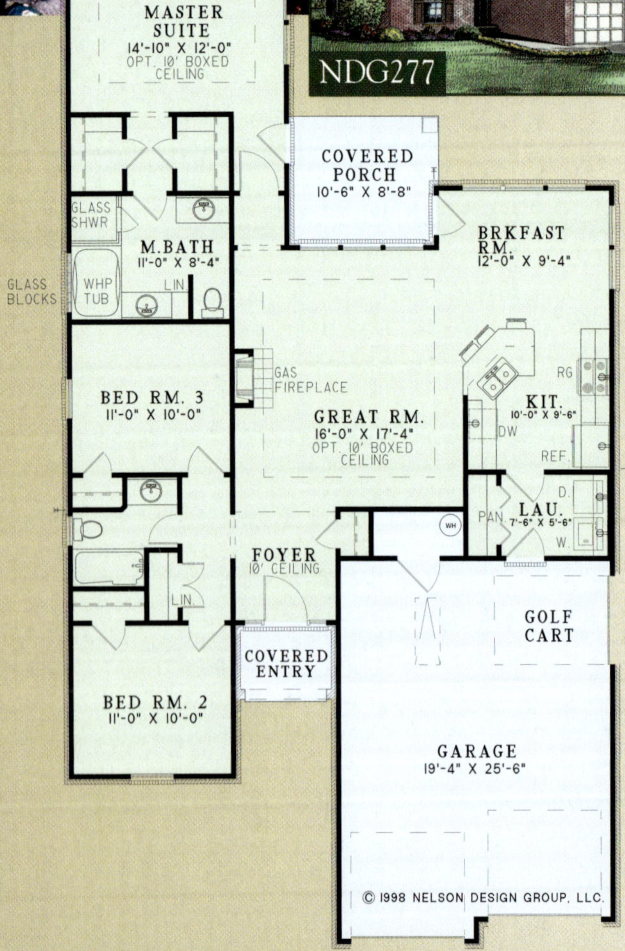

282 Sage Meadows

Width: 38' 4"
Depth: 68' 6"
Total Living: 1379 sq. ft.
Main Ceiling: 9 ft.

Bedrooms: 3
Baths: 2
Foundation: Crawl, Slab,
Plan Options: page 93

Price Tier: A

RENAISSANCE™

A FRENCH COUNTRY NEIGHBORHOOD

6 Featuring NDG Plans

Six beautiful home plans representing the European countryside. They range between 1,850 to 2,300 in square footage - perfect for a growing family!

NDG520

NDG545

NDG519

NDG522

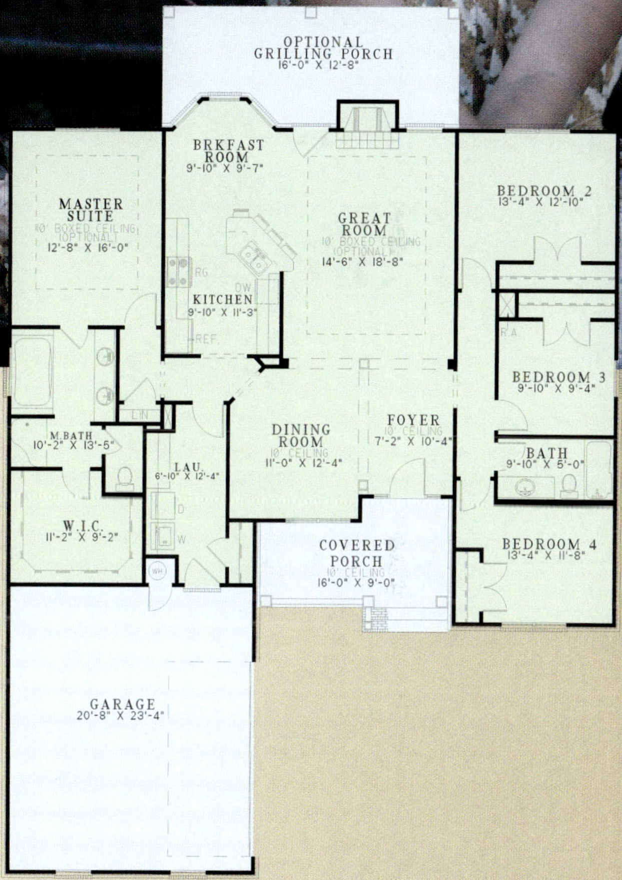

522 Calais Drive

Width: 52' 0"
Depth: 71' 6"
Total Living: 1,930 sq. ft.
Main Ceiling: 9 ft.
Bedrooms: 4
Baths: 2

Foundation: Crawl, Slab, Optional Basement, Optional Daylight Basement
Plan Options: page 93

Price Tier: B

NDG Home Plans for Builders -1st Release 2005

The Multi-Family Collection™

Featuring Over 50 NDG Plans

Multi-family plans featuring more than fifty duplex and triplex designs with a variety of exterior styles and units ranging between 800 to almost 2,500 in square footage.

NDG489

NDG455

NDG792

Home 1 Main Floor Home 2

NDG984

Upper Floor

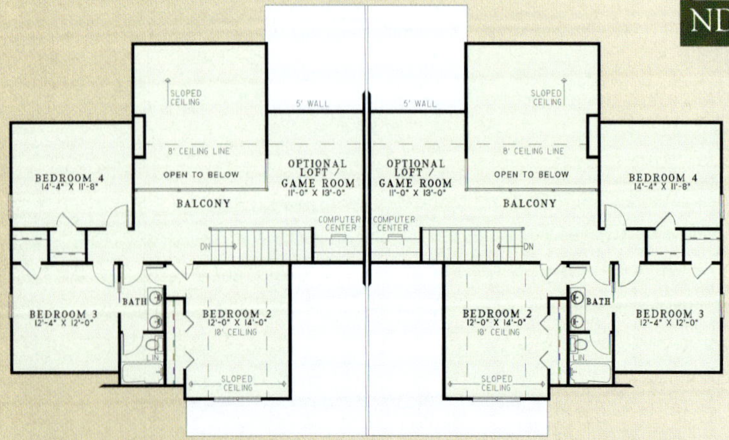

984 Cambridge Court

Width: 83' 71/2"
Depth: 55' 6"
Home 1-
Main Floor: 1,449 sq. ft.
Upper Floor: 795 sq. ft.
Total Living: 2,244 sq. ft.*
***Bonus:** 181 sq. ft.
Combined Living: 4,488 sq.ft.
Main Ceiling: 9 ft.
Upper Ceiling: 8 ft.
Bedrooms: 4
Baths: 2 **Half Baths:** 1
Foundation: Crawl, Slab, Optional Basement, Optional Daylight Basement
Plan Options: page 93

Price Tier: G

To view all the plans in these collections visit www.nelsondesigngroup.com

The Waterfront Collection™

12 Featuring NDG Plans

Beachfront or a golf-course will make the perfect setting for any of these twelve luxurious plans. Living spaces range from 1,400 to 6,500 square feet.

NDG231 - Rear

NDG226 - Rear

NDG311- Rear

NDG173

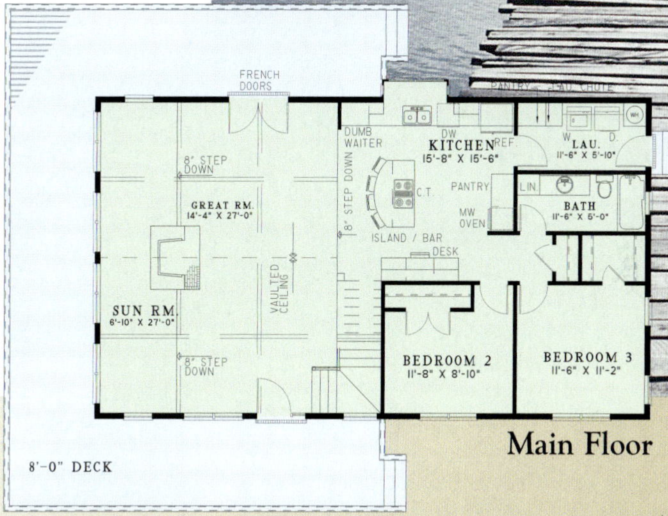

Main Floor

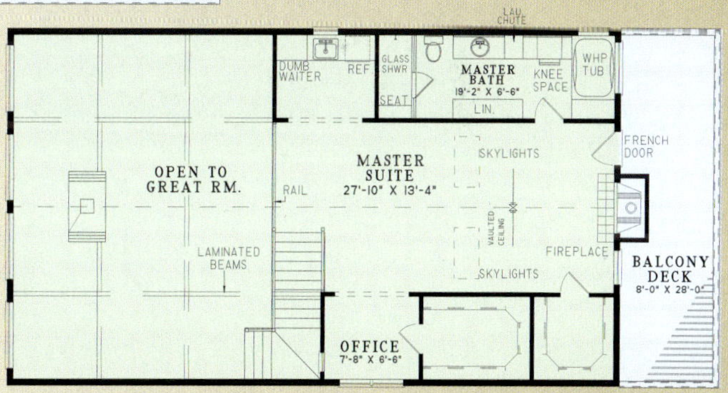

Upper Floor

173 Waterfront Cove

Width: 50' 0"
Depth: 28' 0"
Main Floor: 1,400 sq. ft.
Upper Floor: 743 sq. ft.
Total Living: 2,143 sq. ft.
Main Ceiling: 8 ft.
Upper Ceiling: 8 ft.

Bedrooms: 3
Baths: 2
Foundation: Crawl, Slab, Optional Basement, Optional Daylight Basement
Plan Options: page 93

Price Tier: C

THE *Florida* COLLECTION™

12 Featuring NDG Plans

Enjoy an oasis of amenities in any of these twelve designs created for warmer climates. Plans range between 1,800 to 3,600 square feet with open floor plans and high ceilings.

The Austin - NDG556

The Windsor - NDG551

The Clarion - NDG561

The Evandale - NDG552

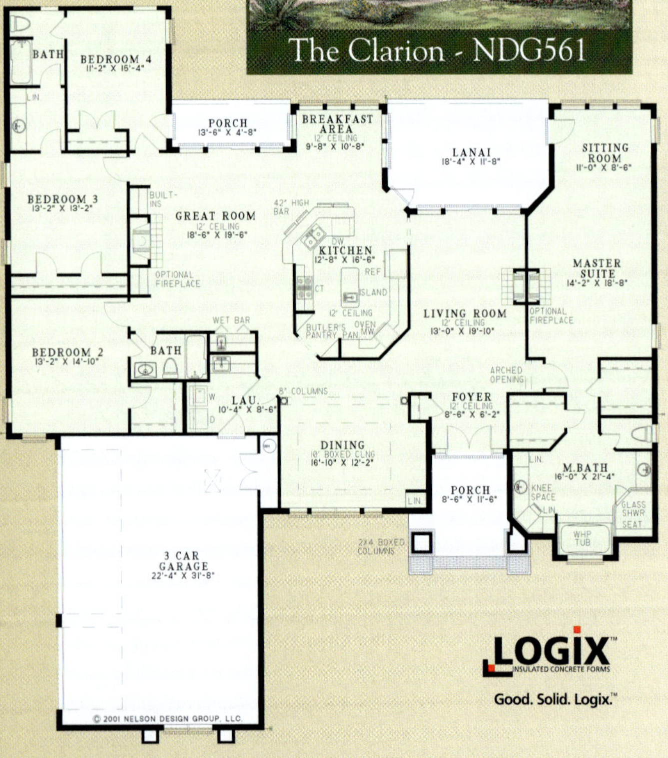

The Evandale

Width: 74' 2"	**Bedrooms:** 4
Depth: 81' 2"	**Baths:** 3
Total Living: 3,021 sq. ft.	**Foundation:** Slab
Main Ceiling: 9' 4"	**Plan Options:** page 93

Price Tier: E

To view all the plans in these collections visit www.nelsondesigngroup.com

THE River Bend™ COLLECTION

Featuring 14 NDG Plans

Fourteen unique designs that range from 1,100 to 1,900 square feet featuring lofts and open floor plans. Make memories that last a lifetime in your River Bend hideaway.

Canoe Point - NDG418

Moss Cove - NDG624

Bluff's Edge - NDG419

Creek Side - NDG415

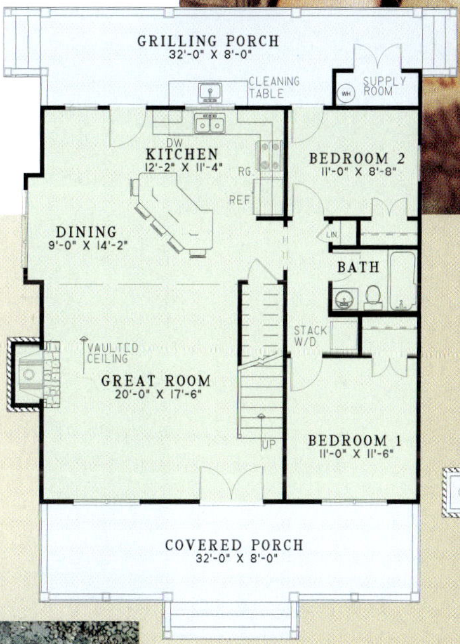

Main Floor

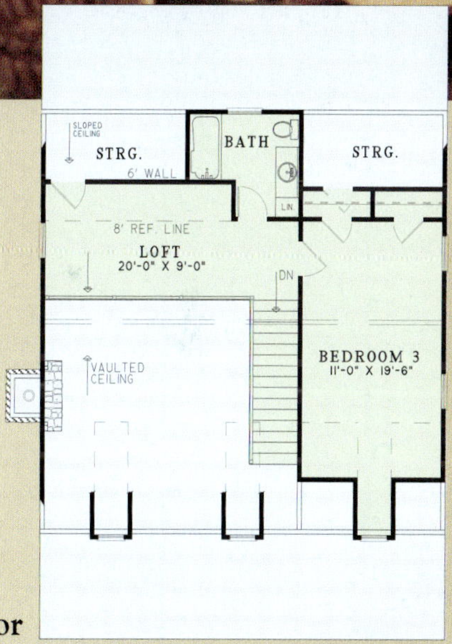

Upper Floor

Creek Side

River Bend Collection I

Width: 34' 4"	**Bedrooms:** 3
Depth: 48' 4"	**Baths:** 2
Main Floor: 1,031 sq. ft.	**Foundation:** Crawl, Slab, Optional Basement, Optional Daylight Basement
Upper Floor: 513 sq. ft.	
Total Living: 1,544 sq. ft.	
Main Ceiling: 8 ft.	**Plan Options:** page 93
Upper Ceiling: 8 ft.	

Price Tier: B

Stone Village™

7 Featuring NDG Plans

A group of seven narrow-lot line home plans ranging from 1,200 to 1,800 square feet. The exteriors are enhanced with natural stone, shutters and arched carriage style garage doors - adding a bit of European country style.

NDG828

NDG825

NDG831

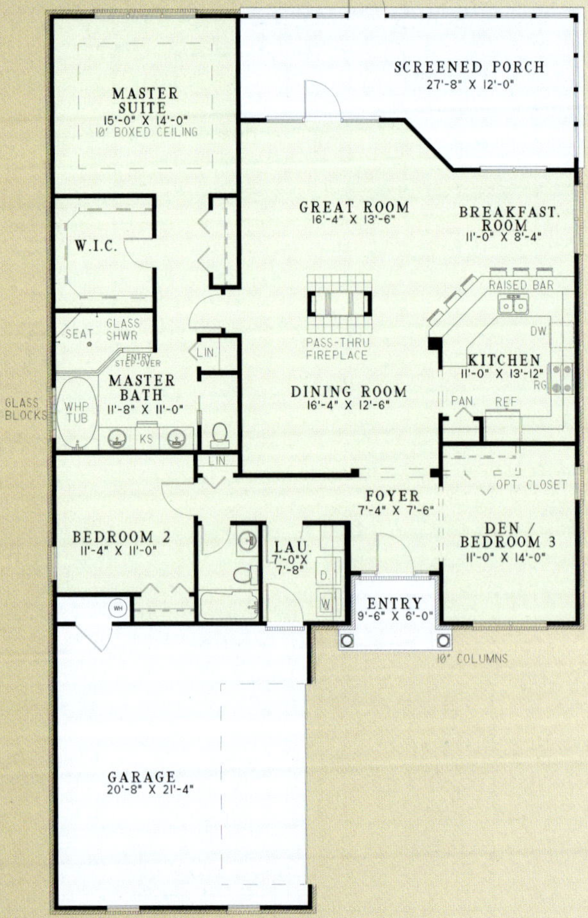

NDG827

827 Woodland Drive

Width: 43' 8"
Depth: 71' 6"
Total Living: 1,806 sq. ft.
Main Ceiling: 9 ft.
Bedrooms: 3
Baths: 2

Foundation: Crawl, Slab, Optional Basement, Optional Daylight Basement
Plan Options: page 93

Price Tier: B

 To view all the plans in these collections visit www.nelsondesigngroup.com

5 Featuring NDG Plans

A sampling of fresh traditional designs with cozy porches and rear-load garages. These narrow lot plans have living spaces of 2,200 to 3,000 square feet that feature media and computer centers.

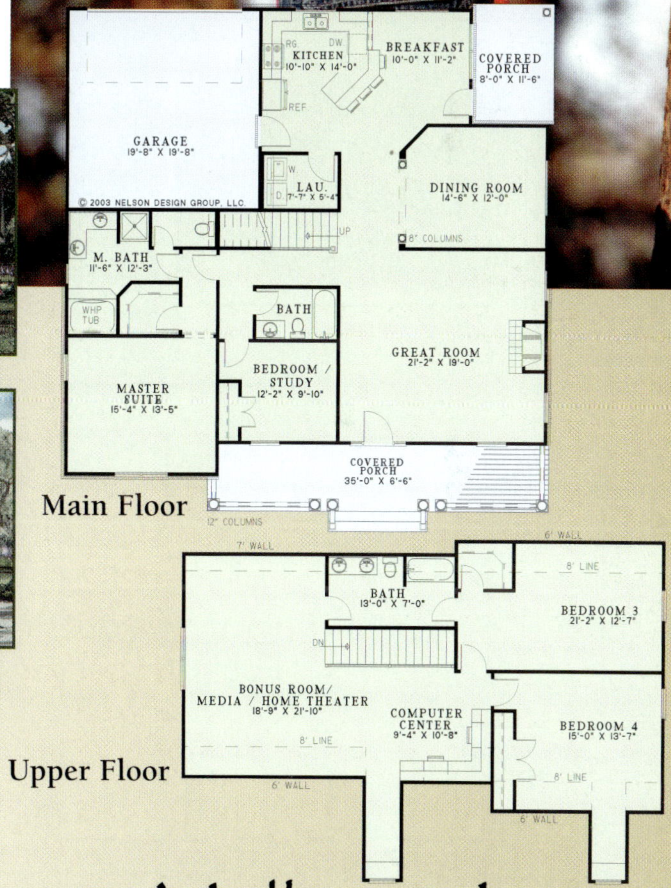

819 Mulberry Lane

Width: 50' 0"
Depth: 50' 0"
Main Floor: 1,733 sq. ft.
Upper Floor: 1,269 sq. ft.
Total Living: 3,002 sq. ft.
Bedrooms: 4
Baths: 3

Main Ceiling: 9 ft.
Upper Ceiling: 8 ft.
Foundation: Crawl, Slab
Plan Options: page 93

Price Tier: E

Aronson Mediterranean™ Collection

50 Premiering more than NDG Plans

These Mediterranean styles of homes with open floor plans have numerous amenities with a various range of square footage offerings – perfect for the coast.

NDG1502

NDG1503

NDG1504

NDG1501

1501 Bayview Drive

Width: 70' 0"
Depth: 88' 6"
Total Living: 3,442 sq. ft.
Main Ceiling: 10 ft.
Bedrooms: 4
Baths: 3 1/2

Foundation: Slab
Plan Options: page 93

Price Tier: E

To view all the plans in this collection visit www.nelsondesigngroup.com

Every day, in communities across the country, more and more homebuyers are leaving conventional 'cookie-cutter' developments in search of something special. In increasing numbers, discerning buyers are choosing log homes for their warmth, beauty and natural charm.

When they choose a Jim Barna log home, they get much more – a builder friendly, well engineered building system, low maintenance, energy efficient with a lifetime warranty on all log elements. They also get personalized service, access to experienced log builders and special prices on major home items from financing to fixtures. Maybe that's why BUILDER magazine ranked Jim Barna Log Systems as the #1 log home company in America.*

Welcome to our Neighborhood...of Log Homes

Jim Barna is proud to offer plans and design services through Nelson Design Group by exclusive arrangement. The following pages, plus the plans included on our websites, represent the latest concepts in comfortable living. For the full collection of 56 collaborative plans and ideas, visit nelsondesigngroup.com.

* *(Builder Magazine, May 2002)*

JIMBARNA
LOG SYSTEMS

LOG HOMES TODAY'S CHOICE FOR COMFORTABLE LIVING

No longer mere 'cabins,' today's log homes are built around today's families. Using modern milling techniques and specialized construction methods, solid log homes offer unparalleled structural integrity, keeping your family warm, safe and secure in any climate. And, by featuring all natural elements, from log walls to timber beams and trusses and knotty pine ceilings, Jim Barna log homes are the perfect 'stress relief' for today's busy lifestyle. It's no wonder that log homes are one of the fastest growing trends in the current housing market.

LET THE LIGHT SHINE IN

Cabins used to be small, dark and dreary. Not so today. Homes from Jim Barna Log Systems tend to feature open, spacious rooms, often with vaulted ceilings and lots of glass. Large kitchens, great rooms, porches and decks make our homes great for entertaining friends or just enjoying family, and the perfect choice for "indoor/outdoor living." And the large master suites can be as lavish as you like!

SOUND INVESTMENT

Even with all the features we build into our homes, they are more affordable than one might think. In fact, with infinite choices in styles and amenities, we can offer homes in every price point and budget, from vacation cottages and starter homes for growing families to high-end executive and retirement homes. According to a study done by the National Association of Home Builders, log homes are an excellent investment, appreciating in value at nearly twice the rate of conventional'stick-built' homes. Plus, Jim Barna helps protect your investment with the strongest warranty in the industry - a lifetime warranty on all log elements, and an available 10-year structural warranty from Bonded Builders Home Warranty Association on all other building materials we supply.
Contact your Jim Barna representative for specific details.

BUILDER'S CHOICE – AND CHOICE BUILDERS!

More builders choose Jim Barna Log Systems than any other log home producer. It's not just for the top quality, kiln-dried materials. We offer builders and homebuyers more - more training, more support, and more options. It starts with our special construction school for builders - The Jim Barna Log Home Institute, where builders learn the specialized techniques that give our homes such strength and beauty. We also have a Builder Services Department to give live support to builders during the construction process.

Giving the best builder support brings us the best builders. You can find them on our National Log Builders Registry, where we list the contact information and experience of hundreds of builders who have completed our classes. These builders, from all over the U.S., are listed exclusively for Jim Barna clients needing construction services. No other log home producer can offer such service!

SEE FOR YOURSELF

Discover for yourself the beauty, comfort and affordability of a Jim Barna log home. With so many choices of plans, log styles and options, you're sure to find a home that's just perfect for your family - and your budget. And, with custom design services from Nelson Design Group, we can create an original design just for you.

So, why not take the next step. To speak with a Jim Barna Building Consultant, to find the nearest Jim Barna representative, or to order our full color catalog of plans and information, call 1-800-962-4734. To see our full portfolio of standard plans online, visit either www.jimbarna.com or www.nelsondesigngroup.com. Either way, we look forward to helping you find a new home that is truly something special.

JIMBARNA

LOG SYSTEMS

www.jimbarna.com

builders@jimbarna.com

P.O. Box 4529, Oneida, TN 37841

800-962-4734

The Baxter

Width: 39' 10"
Depth: 39' 8"
Main Floor: 1,059 sq. ft.
Upper Floor: 390 sq. ft.
Total Living: 1,449 sq. ft.
Main Ceiling: 8' 2"

Bedrooms: 2
Baths: 2 1/2
Foundation: Crawl, Optional Basement, Optional Daylight Basement
Plan Options: page 93

Price Tier: A

To order call toll free 1-800-590-2423

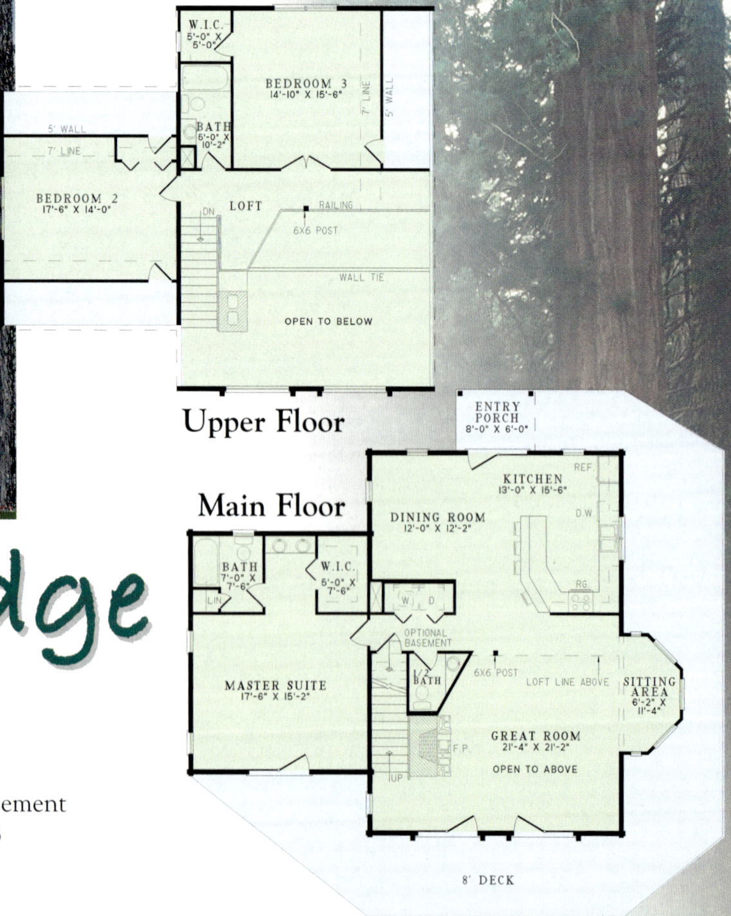

The Eagle Ridge

Width: 54' 0"
Depth: 52' 0"
Main Floor: 1,556 sq. ft.
Upper Floor: 581 sq. ft.
Total Living: 2,137 sq. ft.
Main Ceiling: 8' 2"

Bedrooms: 3
Baths: 2 1/2
Foundation: Crawl, Optional Basement, Optional Daylight Basement
Plan Options: page 93

Price Tier: C

NDG113-1

NDG918

NDG951

NDG761

NDG369

NDG584

Stock Plans

For more than 20 years, Nelson Design Group, LLC has been designing *superior* homes for builders and custom plans for clients throughout the country. As a certified member of the American Institute of Building Designers (AIBD), we are nationally known and have been recognized and *highlighted* in publications such as *HomeStyles Publishing, Home Design Alternatives, Builder Magazine* (the official publication of the National Association of Home Builders), *Home Planners, Architectural Designs, Garlinghouse, Good Housekeeping, Creative Homeowner, Old House Journal, House Beautiful, Better Homes and Gardens,* and *Harris Publications* as well as numerous websites including our own.

A successful and *innovative* company is created by providing the best possible product with creative and knowledgeable people to carry each project to completion. Nelson Design Group, LLC Residential Planners-Designers is one such success.

Our staff of designers offers the qualities a consumer searching for a home desires — experience, creativity and efficiency. We offer *unique* and diversified designs, as well as Southern Traditionals, Lake Houses, Country Styles and Modern Classics. We can modify any of our plans to suit your needs — saving time and guaranteeing customer *satisfaction.*

The following pages reflect some of the stock plans from our portfolio. Visit our web site at **www.nelsondesigngroup.com** for additional plans and new plans that are added continuously.

Nelson Design Group LLC
RESIDENTIAL PLANNERS - DESIGNERS

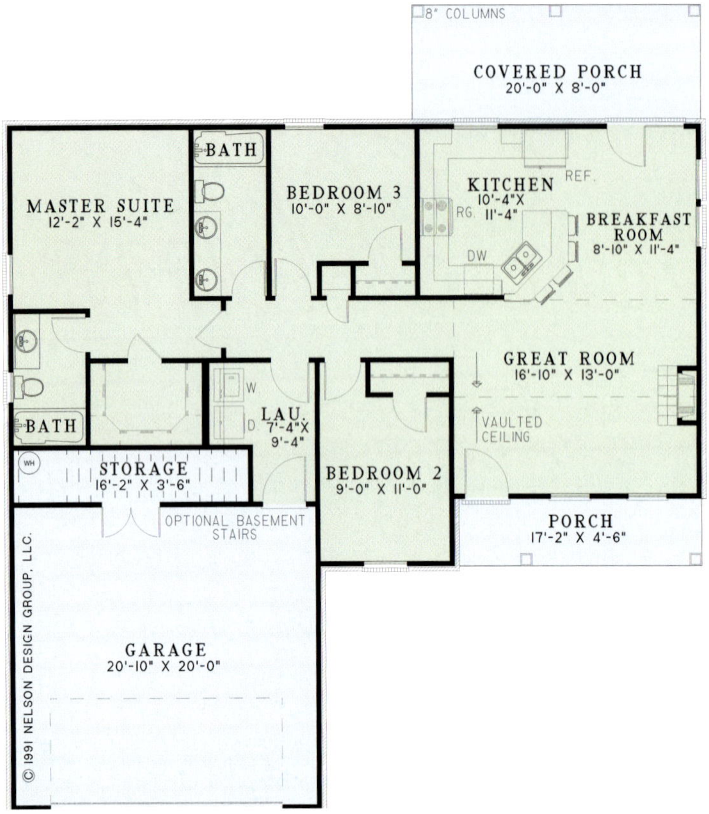

815 Mockingbird Lane

Width: 48' 0"
Depth: 54' 0"
Total Living: 1,193 sq. ft.
Main Ceiling: 8 ft.
Bedrooms: 3
Baths: 2

Foundation: Crawl, Slab, Optional Basement, Optional Daylight Basement
Plan Options: page 93

Price Tier: A

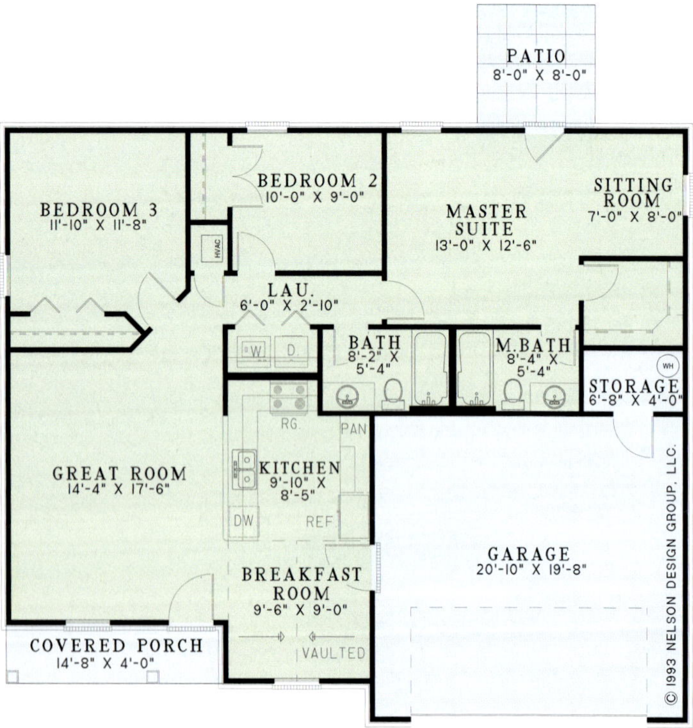

805 Tyler Street

Width: 46' 0"
Depth: 38' 10"
Total Living: 1,214 sq. ft.
Main Ceiling: 8 ft.
Bedrooms: 3
Baths: 2

Foundation: Crawl, Slab, Optional Basement, Optional Daylight Basement
Plan Options: page 93

Price Tier: A

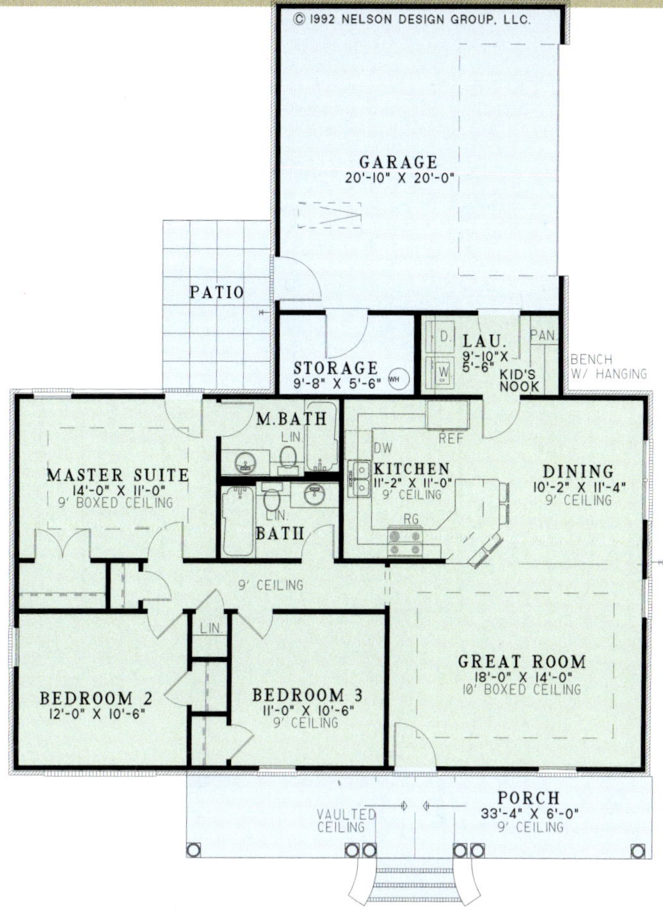

701 Chestnut Lane

Width: 45' 2"
Depth: 59' 0"
Total Living: 1,235 sq. ft.
Main Ceiling: 8 ft.
Bedrooms: 3
Baths: 2

Foundation: Crawl, Slab
Plan Options: page 93

Price Tier: A

Any plan can be modified to your specific needs - Call 1-800-590-2423 for pricing

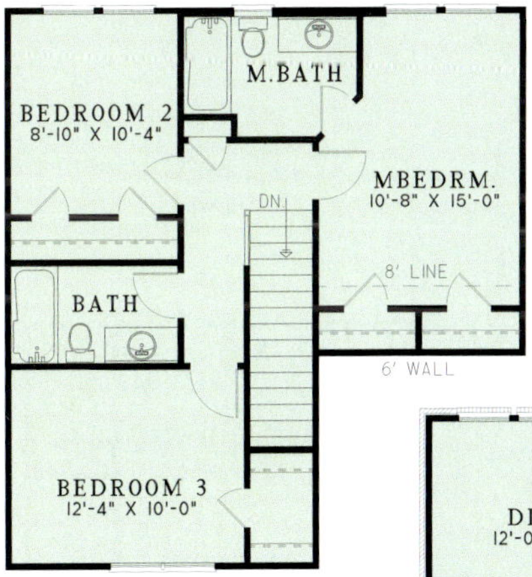

Upper Floor

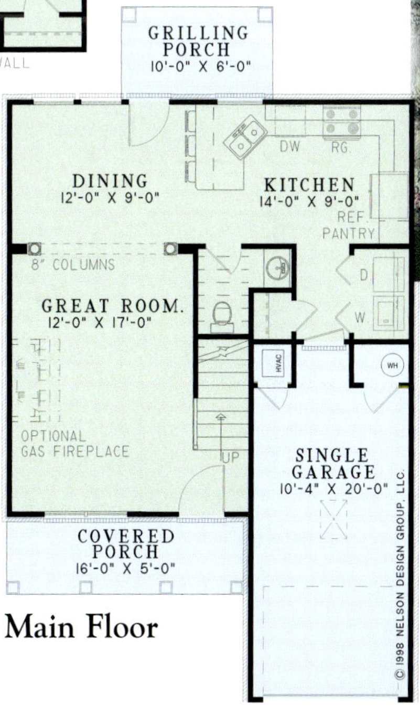

Main Floor

188 Maple Street

Width: 27' 0"
Depth: 45' 0"
Main Floor : 609 sq. ft.
Upper Floor: 642 sq. ft.
Total Living: 1,251 sq. ft.
Main Ceiling: 8 ft.
Upper Ceiling: 8 ft.
Bedrooms: 3
Baths: 2 1/2

Foundation: Crawl, Slab, Basement, Daylight Basement
Plan Options: page 93

Price Tier: A

617 Tyler Street

Width: 48' 4"
Depth: 49' 8"
Total Living: 1,258 sq. ft.
Main Ceiling: 8 ft.
Bedrooms: 3
Baths: 2

Foundation: Crawl, Slab
Plan Options: page 93

Price Tier: A

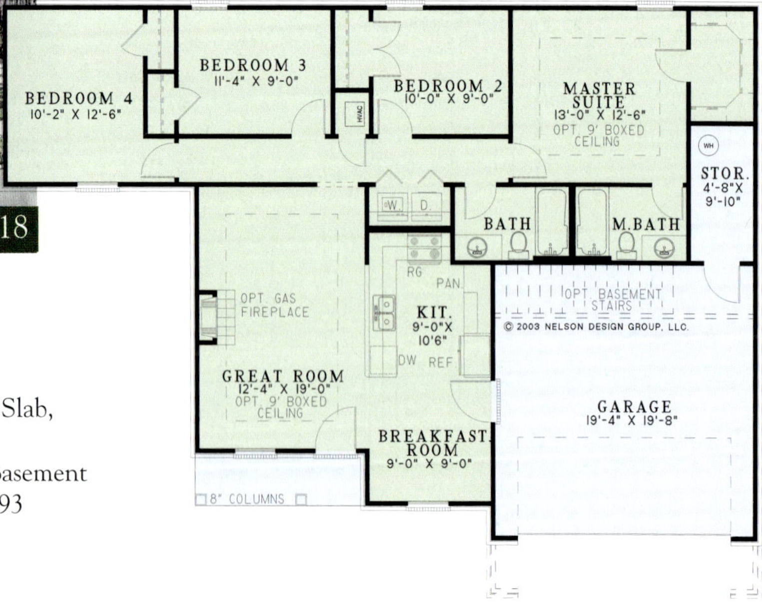

818 Anna Circle

Width: 56' 4"
Depth: 38' 10"
Total Living: 1,271 sq. ft.
Main Ceiling: 8 ft.
Bedrooms: 4
Baths: 2

Foundation: Crawl, Slab, Optional Basement, Optional Daylight Basement
Plan Options: page 93

Price Tier: A

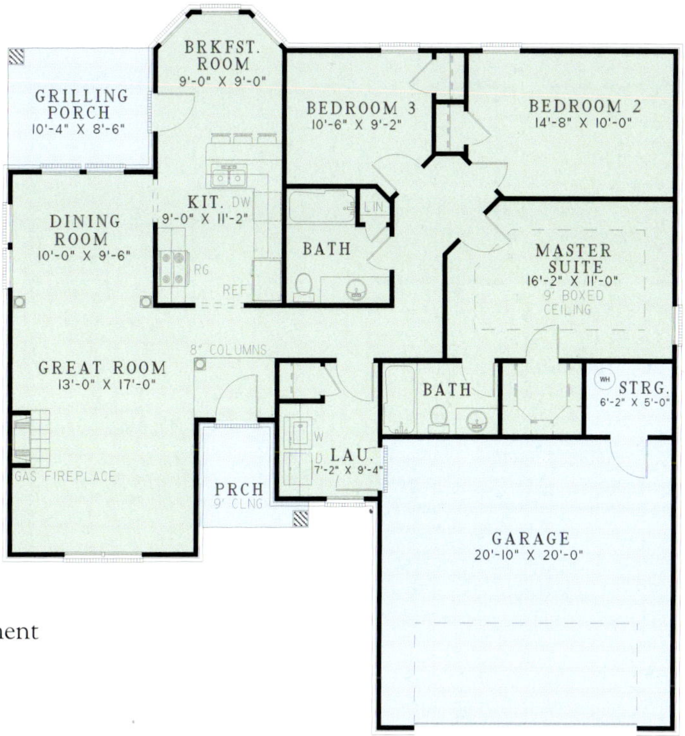

150 Spruce Street

Width: 48' 2"
Depth: 50' 4"
Total Living: 1,353 sq. ft.
Main Ceiling: 8 ft.
Bedrooms: 3
Baths: 2

Foundation: Crawl, Slab, Basement, Daylight Basement
Plan Options: page 93

Price Tier: A

Any plan can be modified to your specific needs - Call 1-800-590-2423 for pricing

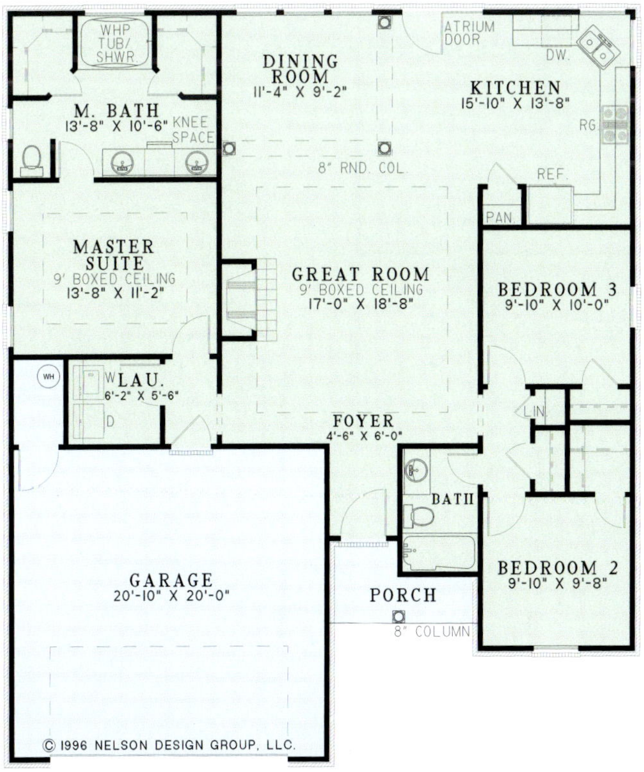

382 Spruce Street

Width: 41' 10"
Depth: 48' 10"
Total Living: 1,382 sq. ft.
Main Ceiling: 8 ft.
Bedrooms: 3
Baths: 2

Foundation: Crawl, Slab, Optional Basement, Optional Daylight Basement
Plan Options: page 93

Price Tier: A

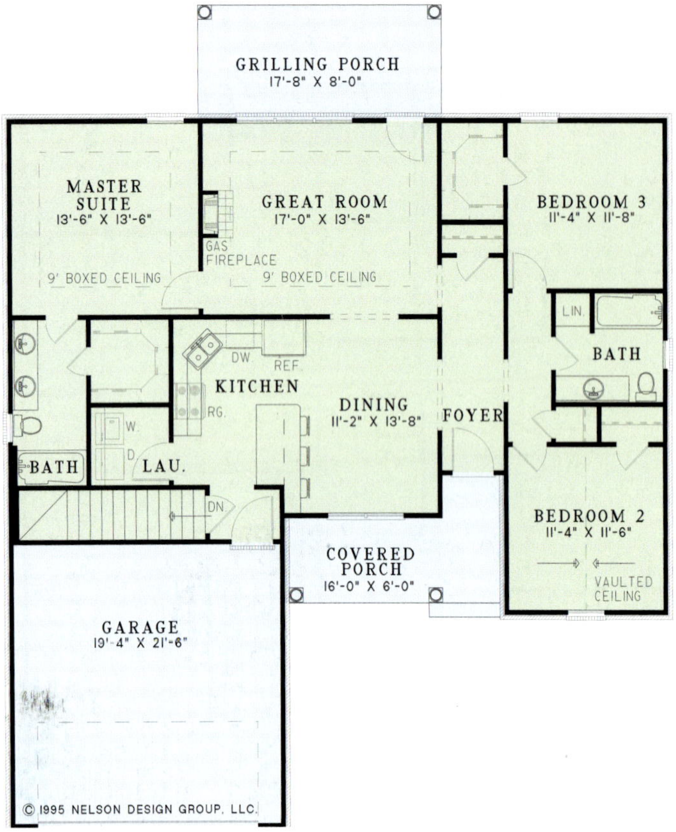

102-2 Spruce Street

Width: 48' 0"
Depth: 58' 0"
Total Living: 1,401 sq. ft.
Main Ceiling: 8 ft.
Bedrooms: 3
Baths: 2

Foundation: Crawl, Slab, Basement, Daylight Basement
Plan Options: page 93

Price Tier: A

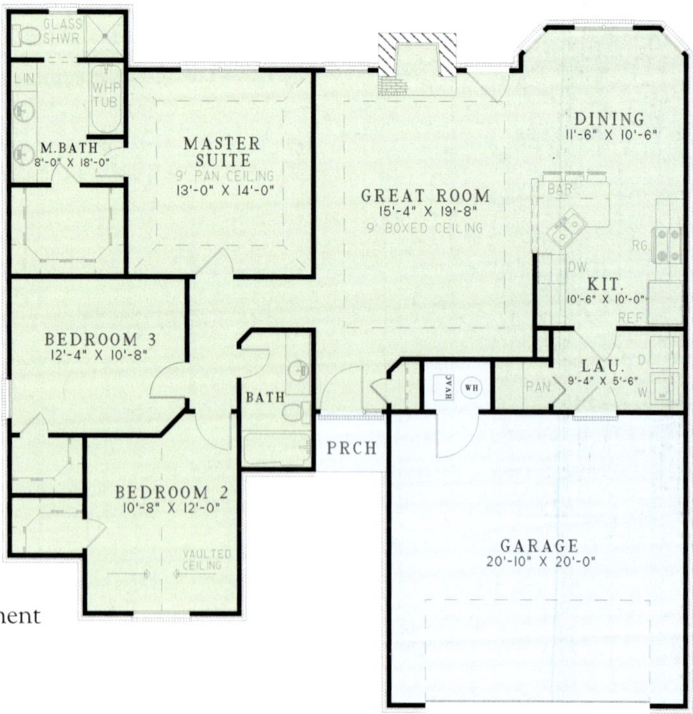

115 Spruce Street

Width: 48' 6"
Depth: 48' 4"
Total Living: 1,461 sq. ft.
Main Ceiling: 8 ft.
Bedrooms: 3
Baths: 2

Foundation: Crawl, Slab, Basement, Daylight Basement
Plan Options: page 93

Price Tier: A

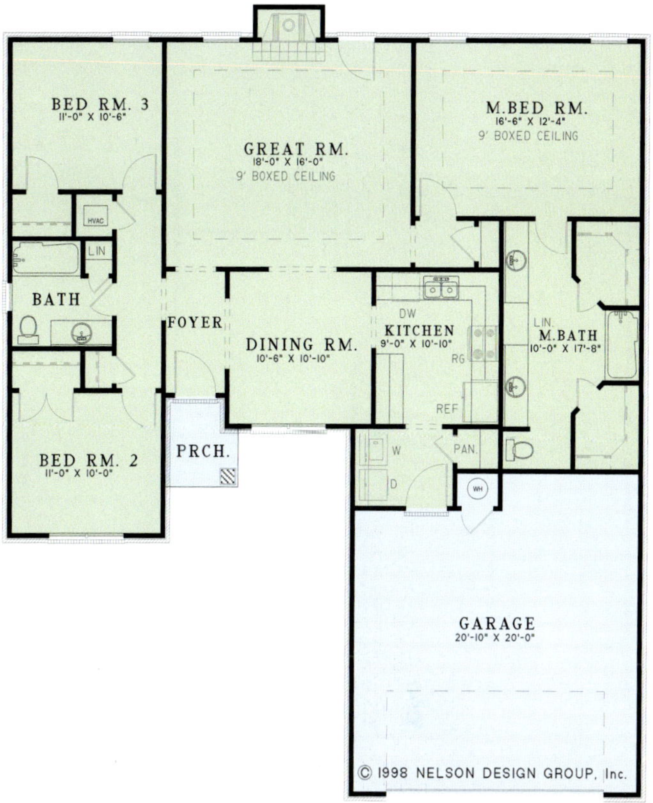

146 Spruce Street

Width: 46' 10"
Depth: 56' 4"
Total Living: 1,474 sq. ft.
Main Ceiling: 8 ft.
Bedrooms: 3
Baths: 2

Foundation: Crawl, Slab, Optional Basement, Optional Daylight Basement
Plan Options: page 93

Price Tier: A

Any plan can be modified to your specific needs - Call 1-800-590-2423 for pricing

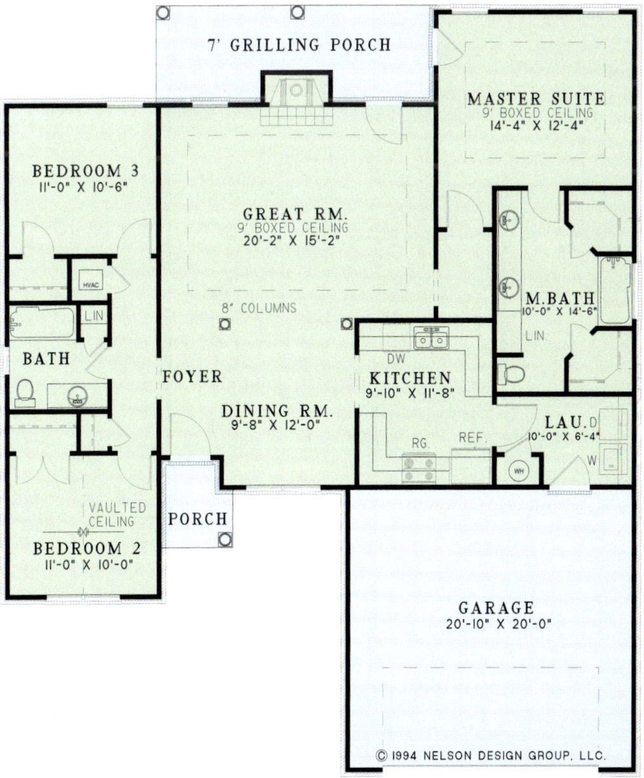

473 Hannah Lane

Width: 46' 10"
Depth: 54' 10"
Total Living: 1,485 sq. ft.
Main Ceiling: 8 ft.
Bedrooms: 3
Baths: 2

Foundation: Crawl, Slab, Optional Basement, Optional Daylight Basement
Plan Options: page 93

Price Tier: A

NDG113-1 Rear Elevation

NDG113-1 Front Elevation

113-1 Chestnut Lane

Width: 51' 6"
Depth: 49' 10"
Total Living: 1,525 sq. ft.
Main Ceiling: 8 ft.
Bedrooms: 3
Baths: 2

Foundation: Crawl, Slab, Basement, Daylight Basement
Plan Options: page 93

Price Tier: B

NDG148

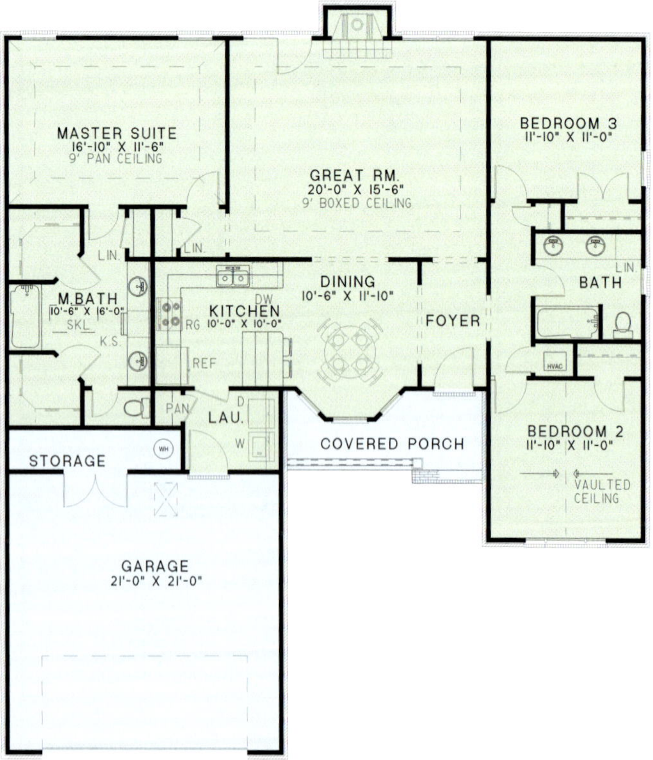

148 Spruce Street

Width: 50' 0"
Depth: 56' 0"
Total Living: 1,538 sq. ft.
Main Ceiling: 8 ft.
Bedrooms: 3
Baths: 2

Foundation: Crawl, Slab, Basement, Daylight Basement
Plan Options: page 93

Price Tier: B

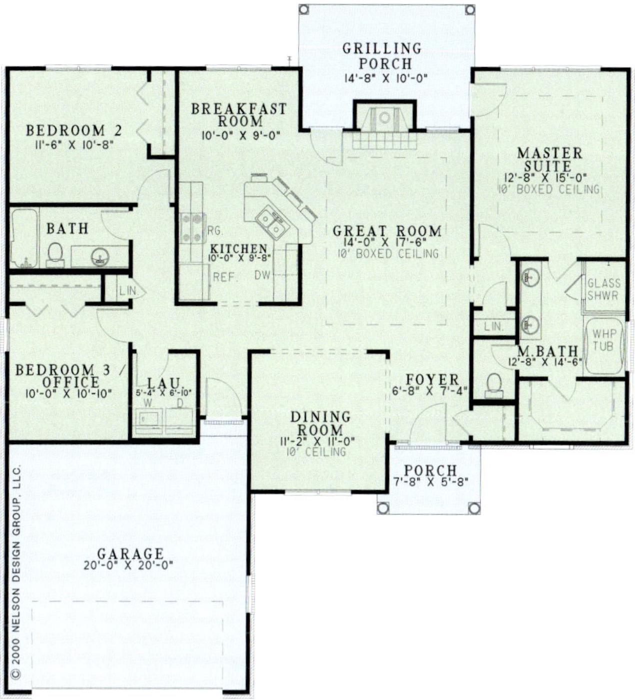

570 Quail Drive

Width: 52' 2"
Depth: 55' 8"
Total Living: 1,560 sq. ft.
Main Ceiling: 9 ft.
Bedrooms: 3
Baths: 2

Foundation: Crawl, Slab, Optional Basement, Optional Daylight Basement
Plan Options: page 93

Price Tier: B

Any plan can be modified to your specific needs - Call 1-800-590-2423 for pricing

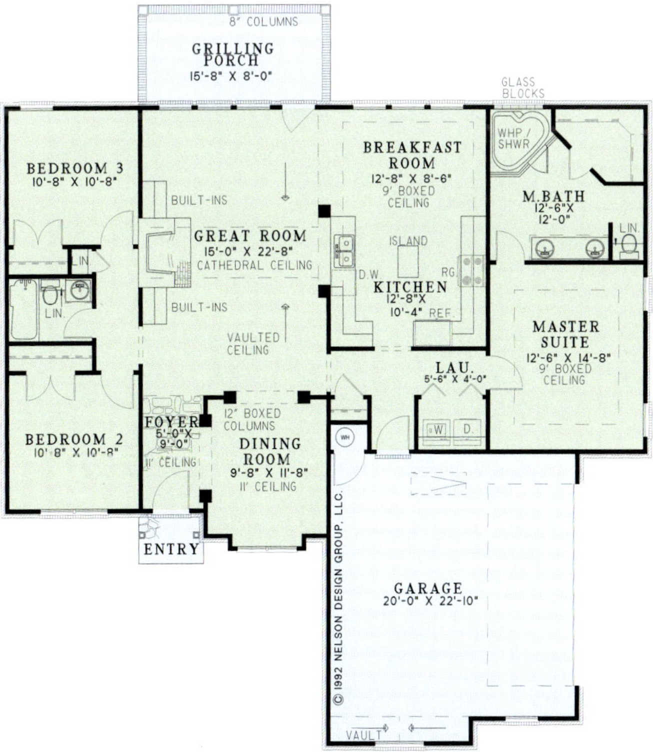

761 Hannah Lane

Width: 52' 6"
Depth: 58' 10"
Total Living: 1,600 sq. ft.
Main Ceiling: 8 ft.
Bedrooms: 3
Baths: 2

Foundation: Crawl, Slab
Plan Options: page 93

Price Tier: B

Main Floor

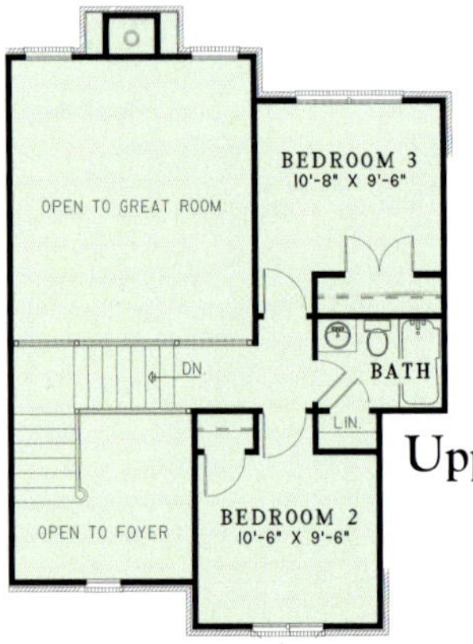

Upper Floor

707 Dogwood Avenue

Width: 56' 6"
Depth: 49' 2"
Main Floor : 1,280 sq. ft.
Upper Floor: 355 sq. ft.
Total Living: 1,635 sq. ft.
Main Ceiling: 8 ft.
Upper Ceiling: 8 ft.

Bedrooms: 3
Baths: 2 1/2
Foundation: Crawl, Slab,
Optional Basement,
Optional Daylight Basement
Plan Options: page 93

Price Tier: B

To order call toll free 1-800-590-2423

165 Willow Lane

Width: 53' 0"
Depth: 59' 10"
Total Living: 1,636 sq. ft.
Main Ceiling: 8 ft.
Bedrooms: 3
Baths: 2

Foundation: Crawl, Slab,
Optional Basement,
Optional Daylight Basement
Plan Options: page 93

Price Tier: B

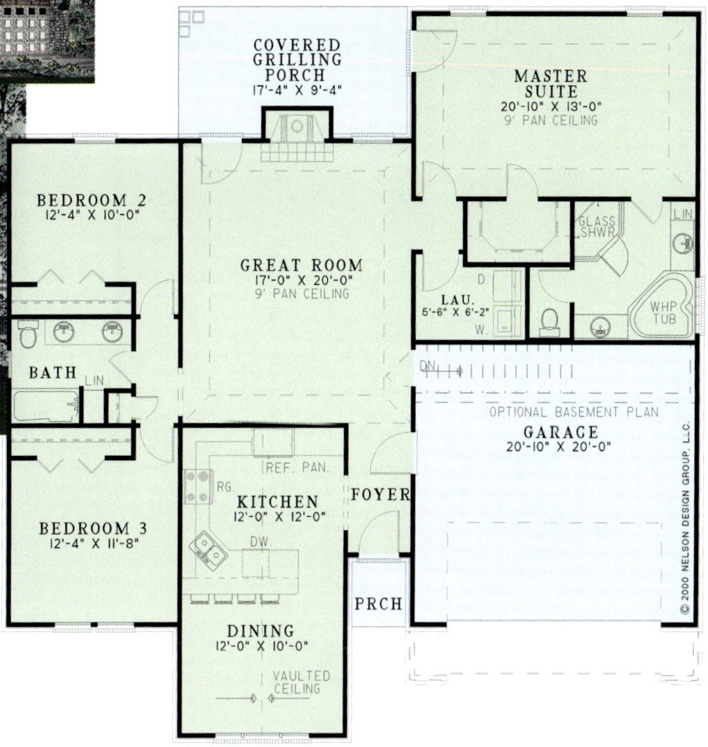

145-2 Spruce Street

Width: 51' 6"
Depth: 52' 4"
Total Living: 1,680 sq. ft.
Main Ceiling: 8 ft.
Bedrooms: 3
Baths: 2

Foundation: Crawl, Slab, Basement, Daylight Basement
Plan Options: page 93

Price Tier: B

Any plan can be modified to your specific needs - Call 1-800-590-2423 for pricing

379 Spruce Street

Width: 58' 0"
Depth: 53' 6"
Total Living: 1,739 sq. ft.
Main Ceiling: 8 ft.
Bedrooms: 3
Baths: 2

Foundation: Crawl, Slab, Basement, Daylight Basement
Plan Options: page 93

Price Tier: B

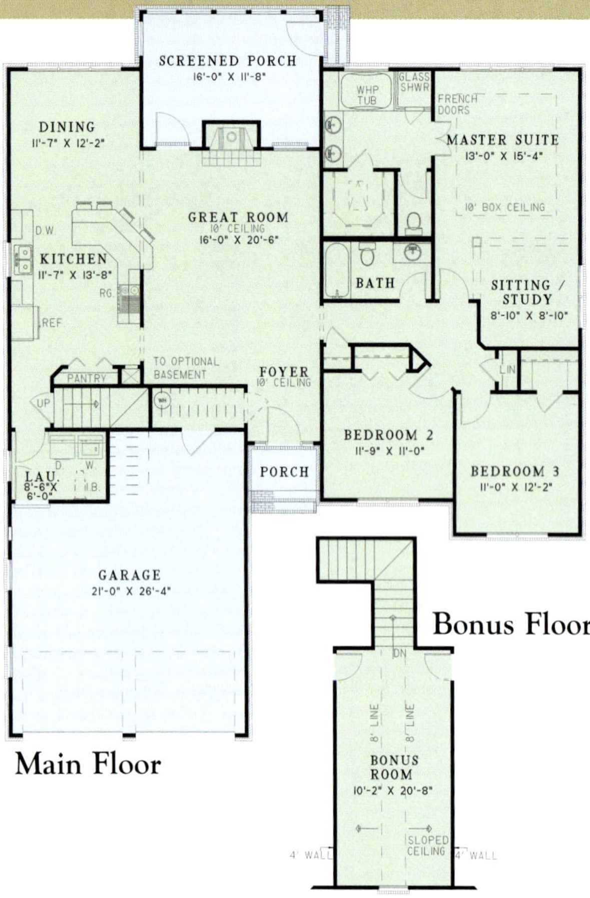

Main Floor

Bonus Floor

NDG507

507 Chestnut Lane

Width: 52' 0"
Depth: 63' 10"
Total Living: 1,732 sq. ft.*
***Bonus:** 243 sq. ft.
Main Ceiling: 9 ft.
Bedrooms: 3
Baths: 2

Foundation: Crawl, Slab, Optional Basement, Optional Daylight Basement
Plan Options: page 93

Price Tier: B

To order call toll free 1-800-590-2423

NDG101-1

NDG101-1B Elevation

101-1 Brighton Court

Width: 39' 0"
Depth: 72' 4"
Total Living: 1,750 sq. ft.
Main Ceiling: 9 ft.
Bedrooms: 3
Baths: 2

Foundation: Crawl, Slab, Basement, Daylight Basement
Plan Options: page 93

Price Tier: B

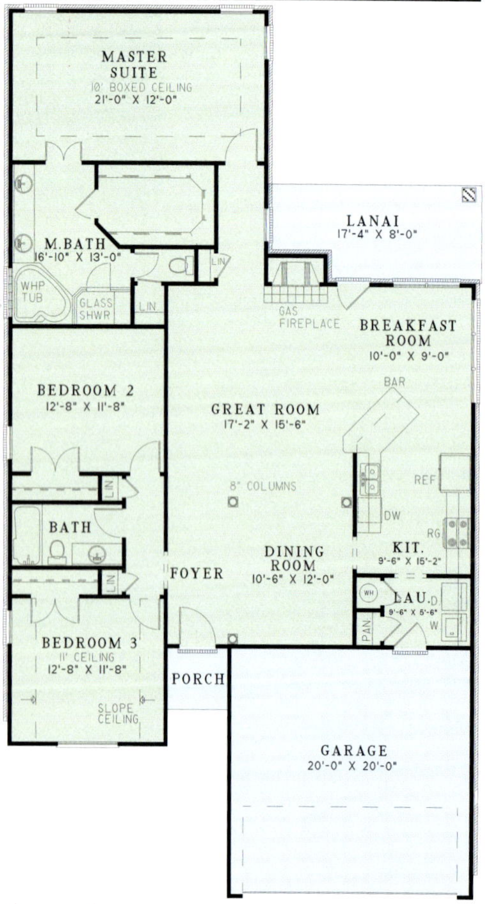

Similar plans can be viewed and ordered at www.nelsondesigngroup.com

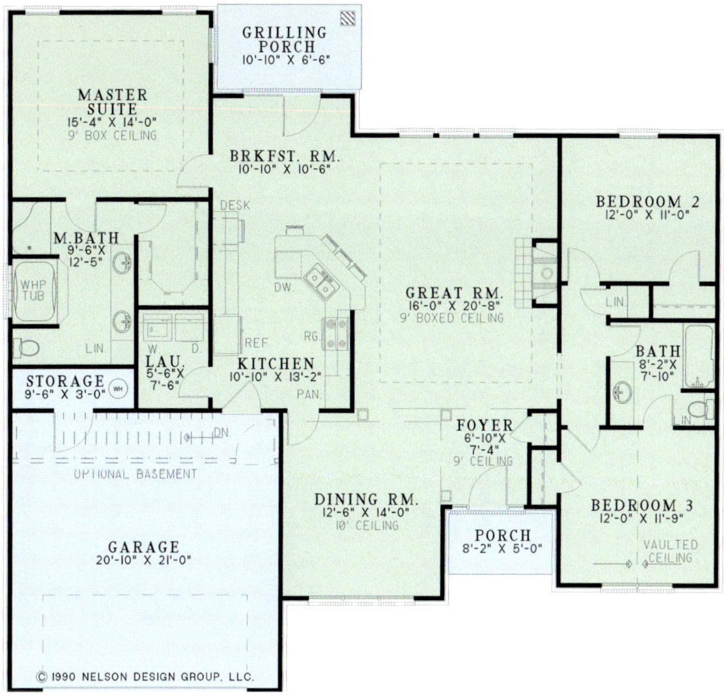

610 Cherry Street

Width: 55' 10"
Depth: 52' 0"
Total Living: 1,763 sq. ft.
Main Ceiling: 8 ft.
Bedrooms: 3
Baths: 2

Foundation: Crawl, Slab, Optional Basement, Optional Daylight Basement
Plan Options: page 93

Price Tier: B

917 Olive Street

Width: 89' 0"
Depth: 49' 4"
Total Living: 1,800 sq. ft.
Main Ceiling: 8 ft.
Bedrooms: 3
Baths: 2
Foundation: Crawl, Slab
Plan Options: page 93

Price Tier: B

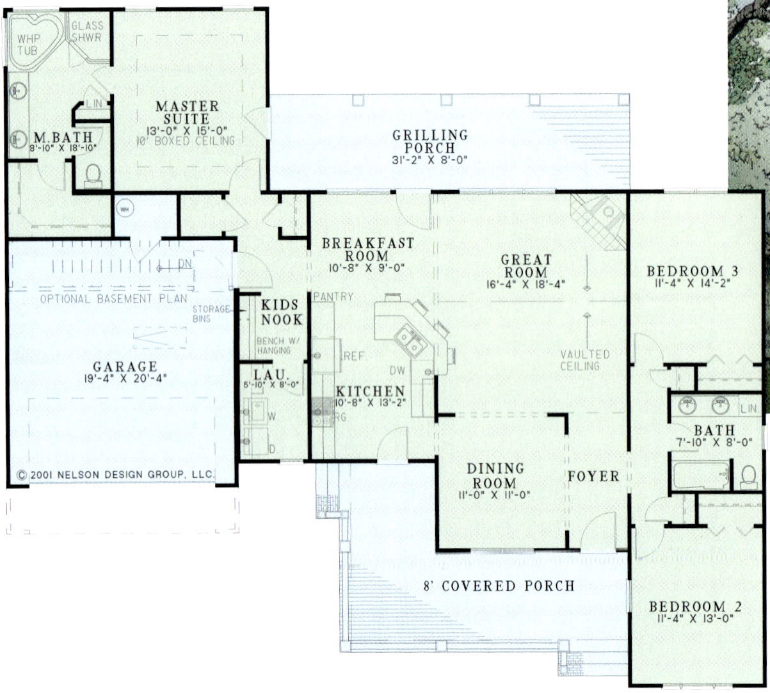

567 Thomas Road

Width: 65' 8"
Depth: 57' 0"
Total Living: 1,813 sq. ft.
Main Ceiling: 9 ft.
Bedrooms: 3
Baths: 2

Foundation: Crawl, Slab, Optional Basement, Optional Daylight Basement
Plan Options: page 93

Price Tier: B

To order call toll free 1-800-590-2423

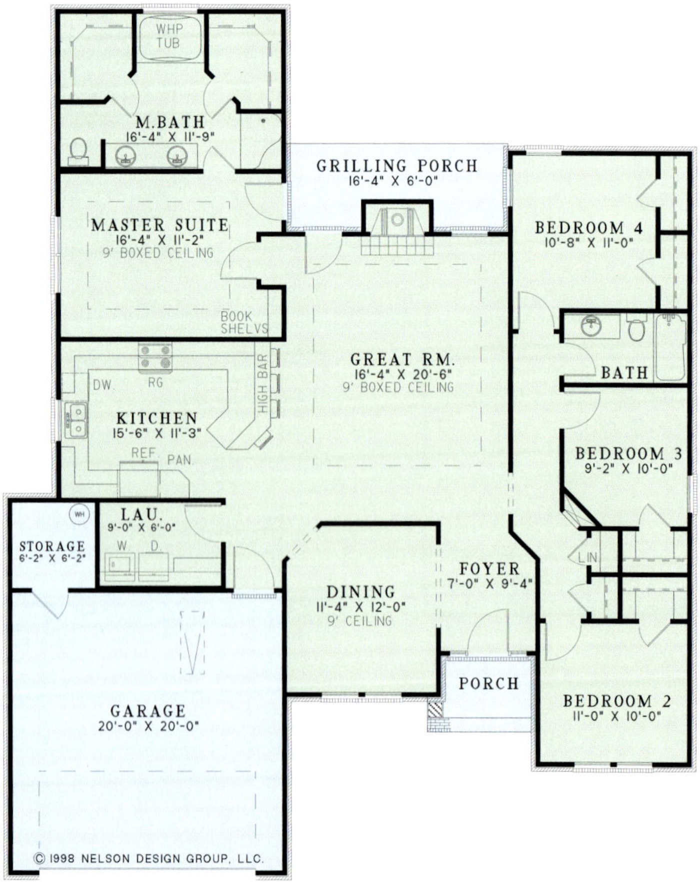

548 Tyler Street

Width: 50' 8"
Depth: 62' 4"
Total Living: 1,832 sq. ft.
Main Ceiling: 8 ft.
Bedrooms: 4
Baths: 2

Foundation: Crawl, Slab, Optional Basement, Optional Daylight Basement
Plan Options: page 93

Price Tier: B

Similar plans can be viewed and ordered at www.nelsondesigngroup.com

Main Floor

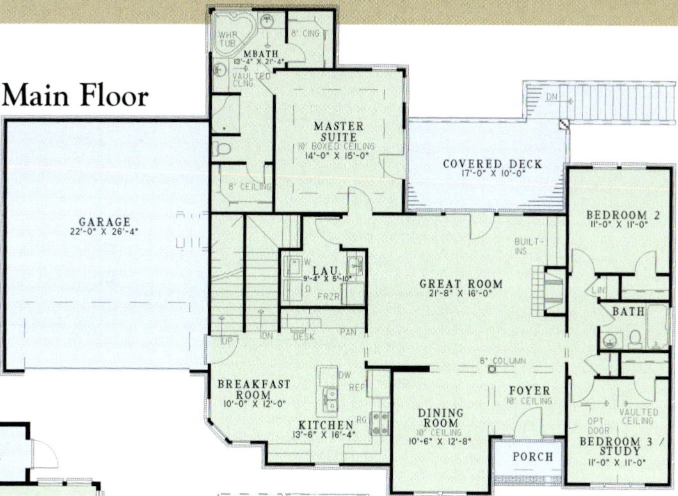

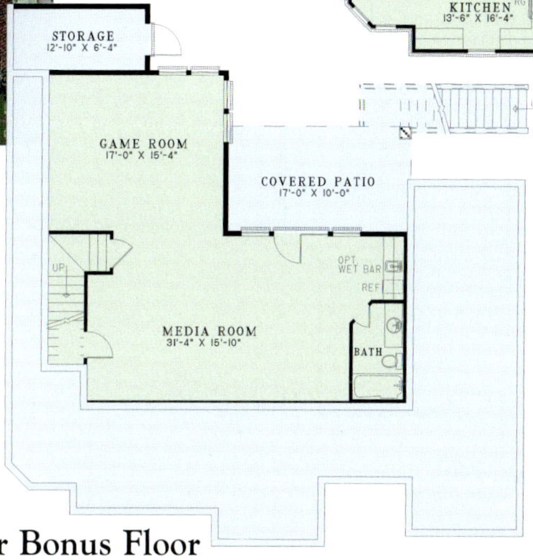

Upper Bonus Floor

Lower Bonus Floor

136 Spruce Street

Width: 73' 4"
Depth: 51' 8"
Total Living: 1,871 sq. ft.*
* Upper Bonus: 390 sq. ft.
* Lower Bonus: 860 sq. ft.
Main Ceiling: 9 ft.
Upper Ceiling: 8 ft.

Bedrooms: 3
Baths: 2
Foundation: Crawl, Slab, Basement, Daylight Basement
Plan Options: page 93

Price Tier: B

Any plan can be modified to your specific needs - Call 1-800-590-2423 for pricing

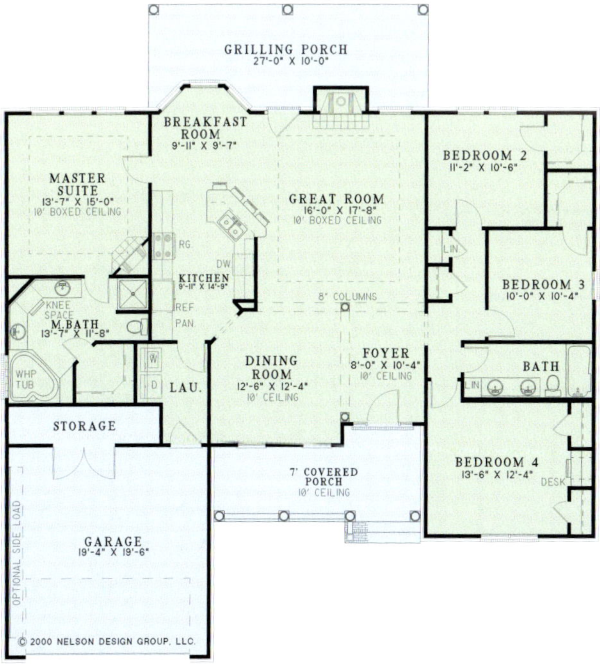

483 Spruce Street

Width: 57' 0"
Depth: 61' 4"
Total Living: 1,880 sq. ft.
Main Ceiling: 9 ft.
Bedrooms: 4
Baths: 2

Foundation: Crawl, Slab, Basement, Daylight Basement
Plan Options: page 93

Price Tier: B

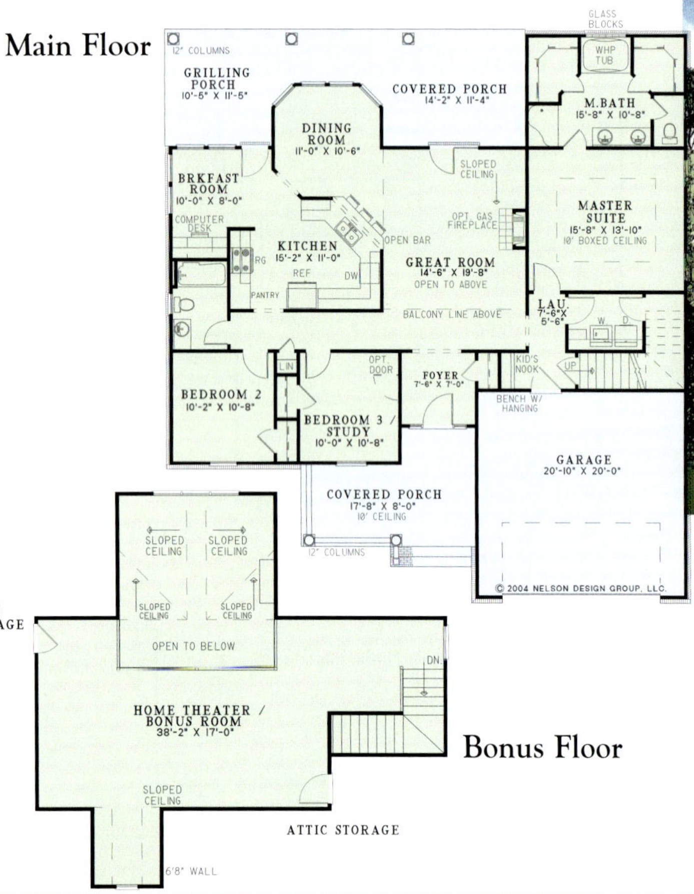

941 Quail Drive

Width: 52' 6"
Depth: 55' 6"
Total Living: 1,710 sq. ft.*
*Bonus: 557 sq. ft.
Main Ceiling: 9 ft.
Bonus Ceiling: 8 ft.
Bedrooms: 3
Baths: 2

Foundation: Crawl, Slab, Optional Basement, Optional Daylight Basement
Plan Options: page 93

Price Tier: B

To order call toll free 1-800-590-2423

702 Cherry Street

Width: 69' 6"
Depth: 44' 4"
Total Living: 1,913 sq. ft.
Main Ceiling: 8 ft.
Bedrooms: 4
Baths: 2
Foundation: Crawl, Slab
Plan Options: page 93

Price Tier: B

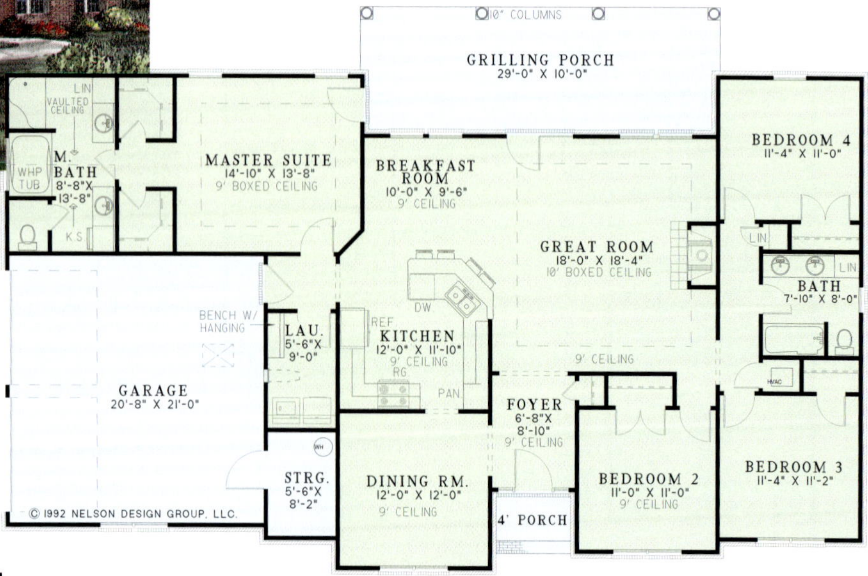

Similar plans can be viewed and ordered at www.nelsondesigngroup.com

Main Floor

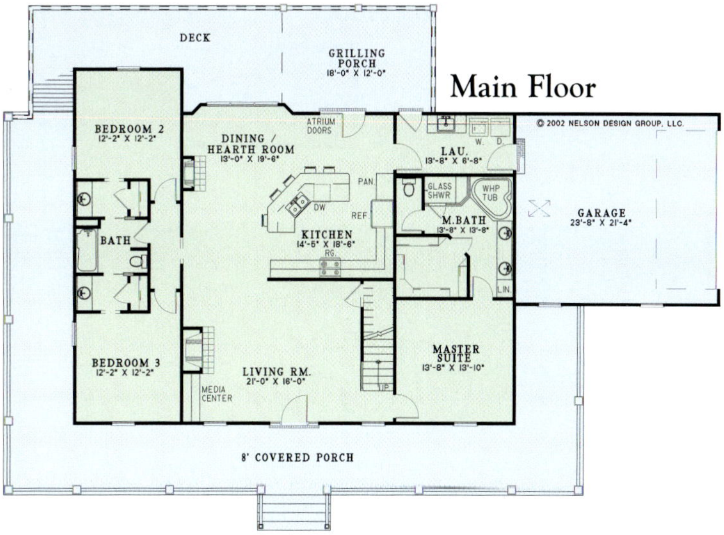

602 *Olive Street*

Width: 84' 0"
Depth: 55' 6"
Total Living: 1,921 sq. ft.*
*Bonus: 812 sq. ft.
Main Ceiling: 8 ft.
Bonus Ceiling: 8 ft.
Bedrooms: 3
Baths: 3

Foundation: Crawl, Slab, Basement, Daylight Basement
Plan Options: page 93

Price Tier: B

Bonus Floor

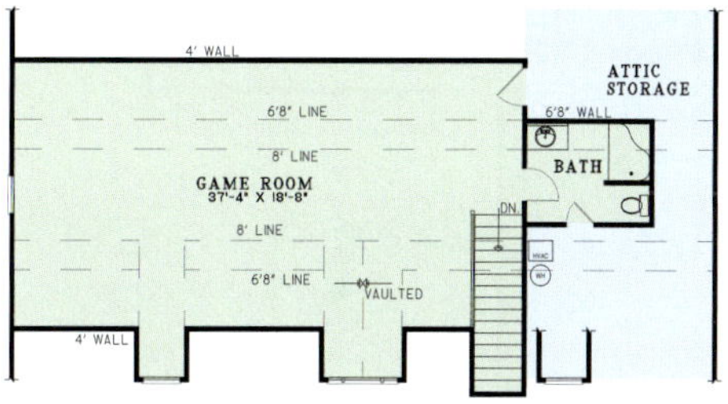

Any plan can be modified to your specific needs - Call 1-800-590-2423 for pricing

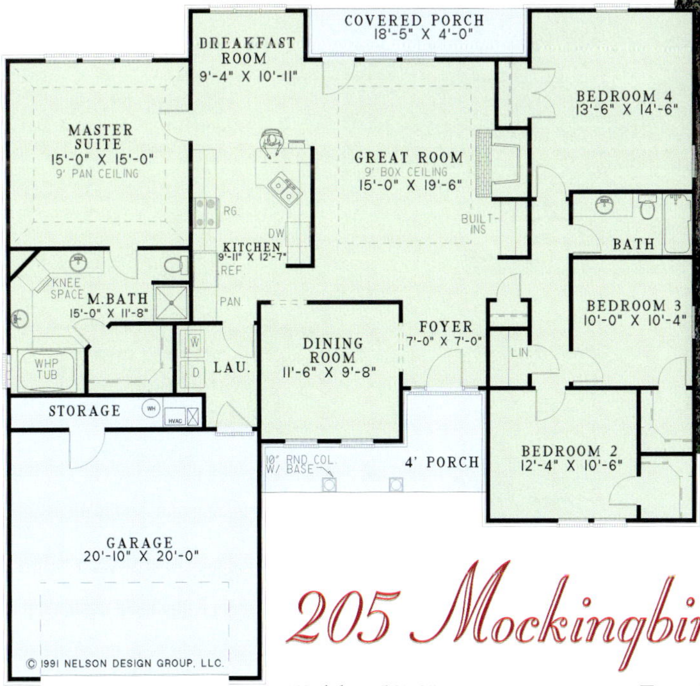

205 *Mockingbird Lane*

Width: 58' 0"
Depth: 54' 10"
Total Living: 1,940 sq. ft.
Main Ceiling: 8 ft.
Bedrooms: 4
Baths: 2

Foundation: Crawl, Slab, Basement, Daylight Basement
Plan Options: page 93

Price Tier: B

Bonus Floor

Main Floor

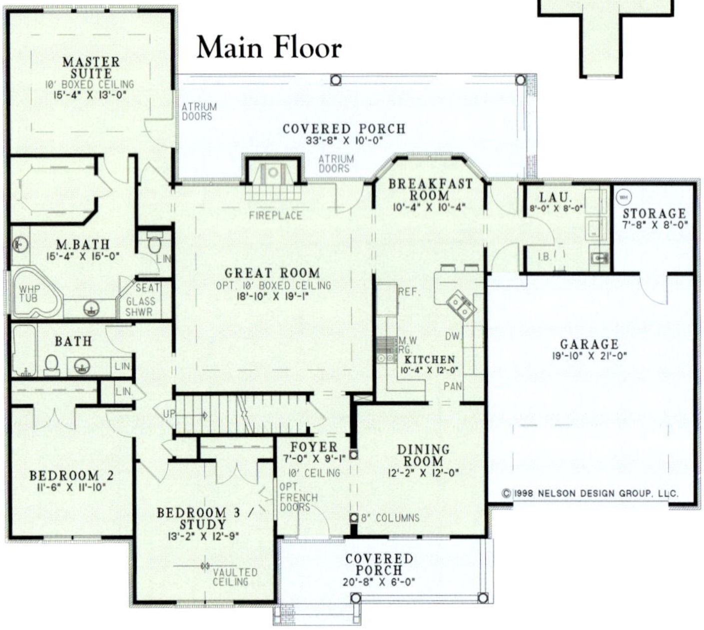

347 Maple Street

Width: 66' 0"
Depth: 55' 0"
Total Living: 1,957 sq. ft.*
*Bonus: 479 sq. ft.
Main Ceiling: 9 ft.
Bonus Ceiling: 8 ft.
Bedrooms: 3
Baths: 2

Foundation: Crawl, Slab, Basement, Daylight Basement
Plan Options: page 93

Price Tier: B

To order call toll free 1-800-590-2423

NDG544B Elevation

Bonus Floor

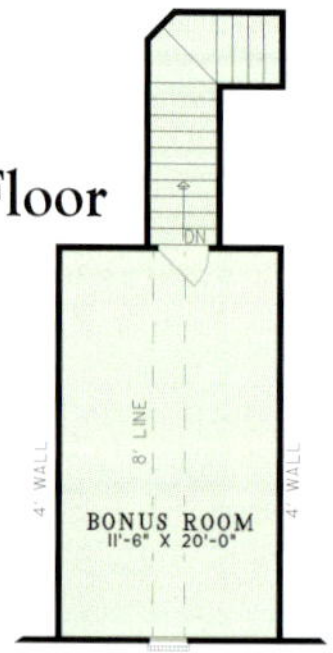

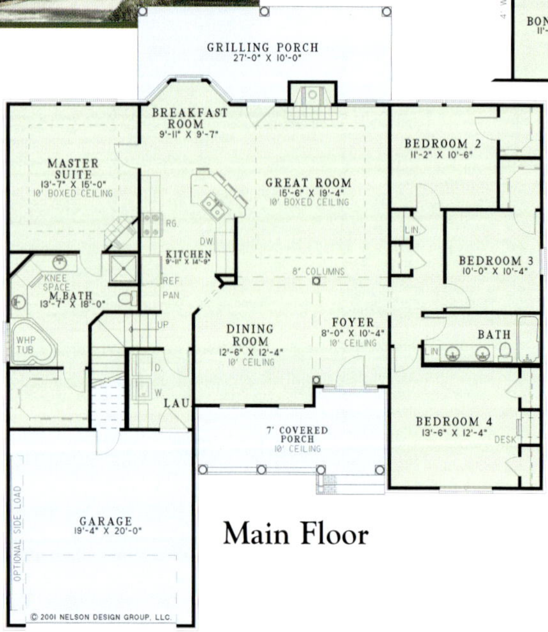

Main Floor

544 Glendale Avenue

Width: 57' 0"
Depth: 64' 4"
Total Living: 1,965 sq. ft.*
*Bonus Floor: 251 sq. ft.
Main Ceiling: 9 ft.
Bedrooms: 4
Baths: 2

Foundation: Crawl, Slab, Optional Basement, Optional Daylight Basement
Plan Options: page 93

Price Tier: B

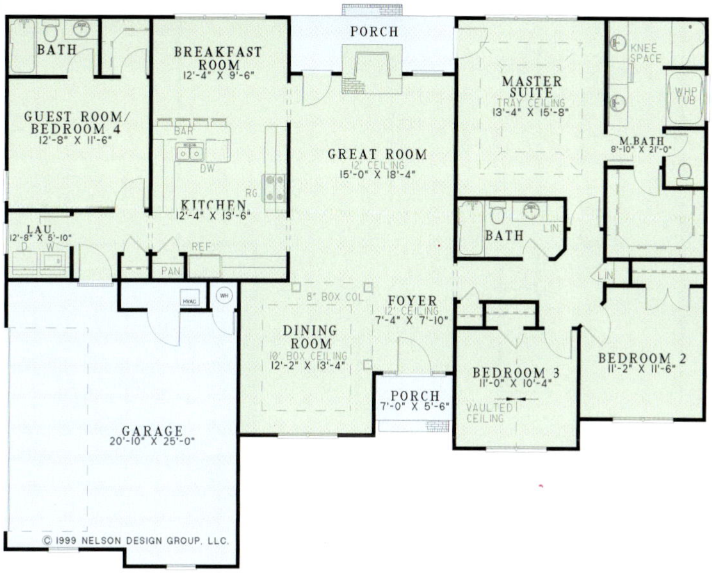

378 Dogwood Avenue

Width: 64' 2"
Depth: 49' 0"
Total Living: 1,989 sq. ft.
Main Ceiling: 9 ft.
Bedrooms: 4
Baths: 3

Foundation: Crawl, Slab, Basement, Daylight Basement
Plan Options: page 93

Price Tier: B

956 Hannah Lane

Width: 59' 0"
Depth: 69' 0"
Total Living: 1,689 sq. ft.
Main Ceiling: 9 ft.
Bedrooms: 3
Baths: 2

Foundation: Crawl, Slab
Plan Options: page 93

Price Tier: B

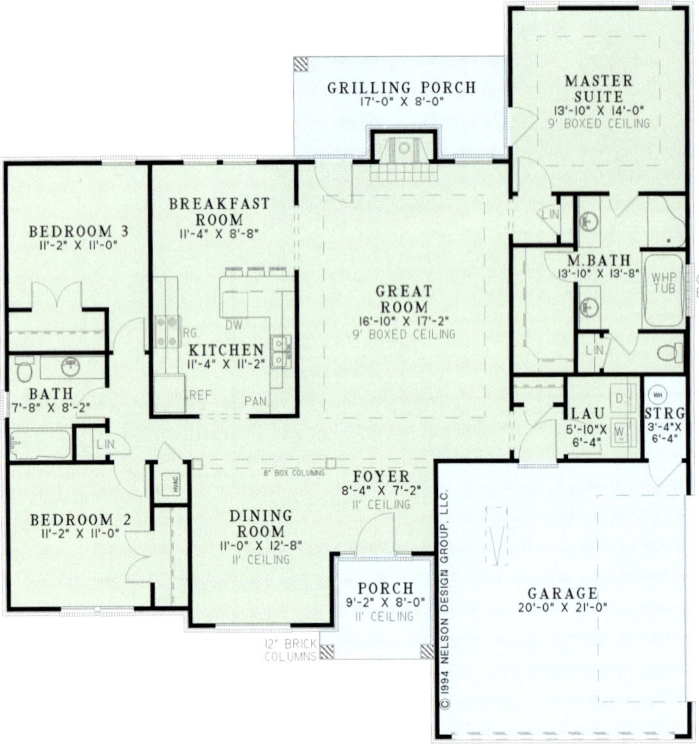

905 Dogwood Lane

Width: 54' 10"
Depth: 56' 8"
Total Living: 1,807 sq. ft.
Main Ceiling: 8 ft.
Bedrooms: 3
Baths: 2

Foundation: Crawl, Slab, Optional Basement, Optional Daylight Basement
Plan Options: page 93

Price Tier: B

To order call toll free 1-800-590-2423

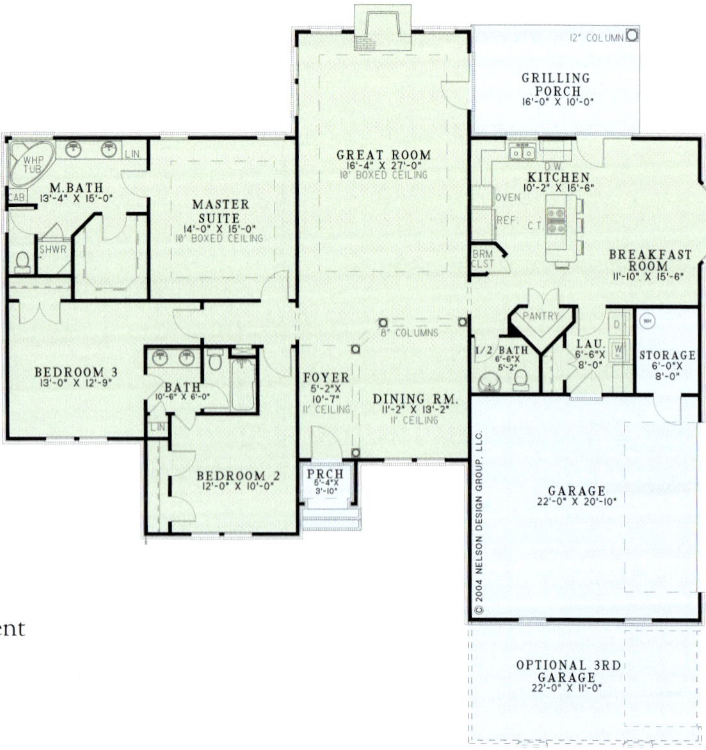

764 Magnolia Drive

Width: 69' 4"
Depth: 58' 2"
Total Living: 2,134 sq. ft.
Main Ceiling: 9 ft.
Bedrooms: 3
Baths: 2 1/2

Foundation: Crawl, Slab, Optional Basement, Optional Daylight Basement
Plan Options: page 93

Price Tier: C

Main Floor

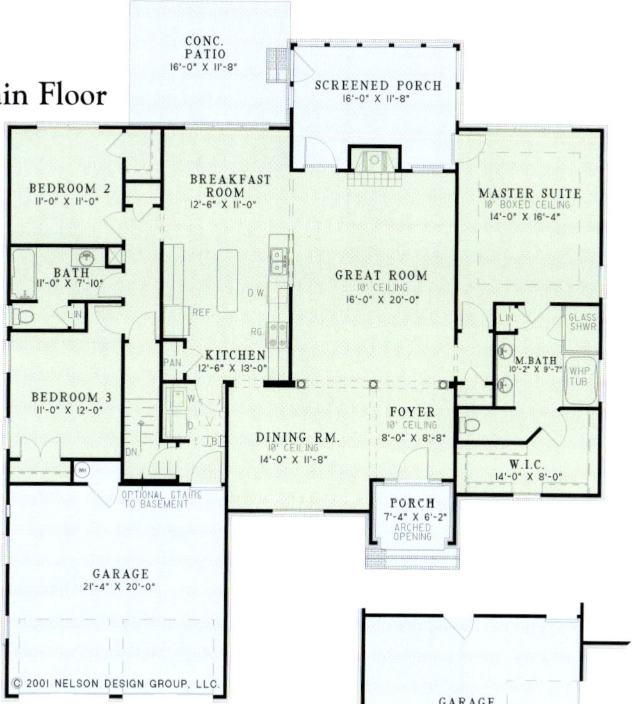

510 Quail Drive

Width: 59' 0"
Depth: 62' 10"
Total Living: 2,014 sq. ft.
Main Ceiling: 9 ft.
Bedrooms: 3
Baths: 2

Foundation: Crawl, Slab, Optional Basement, Optional Daylight Basement
Plan Options: page 93

Price Tier: C

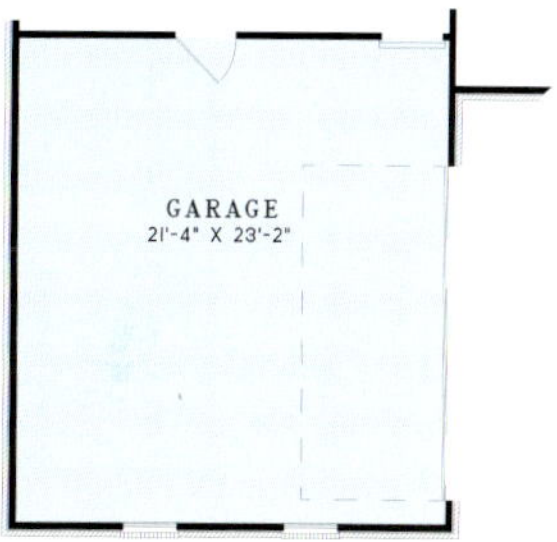

Optional Courtyard Garage

Any plan can be modified to your specific needs - Call 1-800-590-2423 for pricing

517 Belmont Avenue

Width: 64' 2"
Depth: 52' 0"
Total Living: 2,022 sq. ft.
Main Ceiling: 9 ft.
Bedrooms: 4
Baths: 3

Foundation: Crawl, Slab, Optional Basement, Optional Daylight Basement
Plan Options: page 93

Price Tier: C

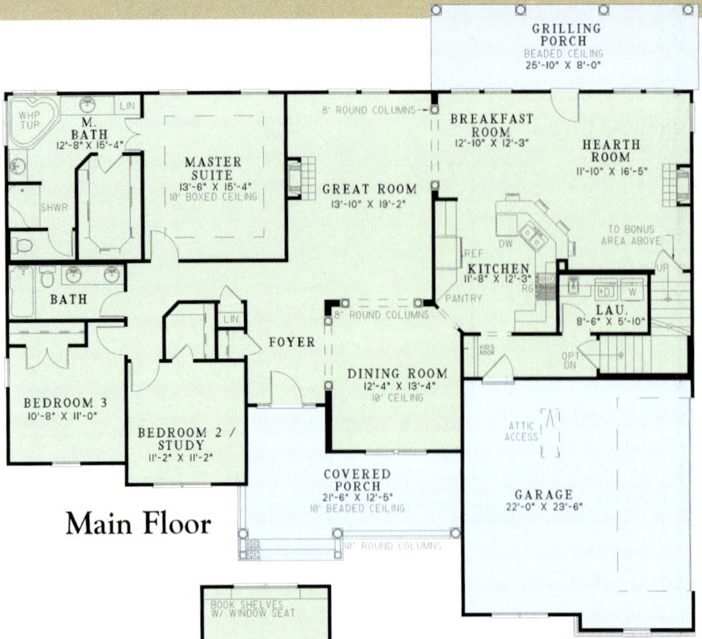

Main Floor

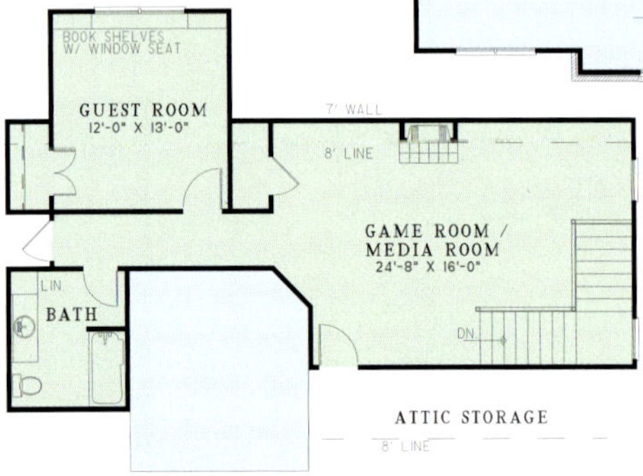

Bonus Floor

472-1 Mockingbird Lane

Width: 66' 4"
Depth: 58' 7"
Total Living: 2,029 sq. ft.*
*Bonus Floor: 754 sq. ft.
Main Ceiling: 9 ft.
Bonus Ceiling: 8 ft.
Bedrooms: 3
Baths: 2

Foundation: Crawl,Slab, Basement, Daylight Basement
Plan Options: page 93

Price Tier: C

To order call toll free 1-800-590-2423

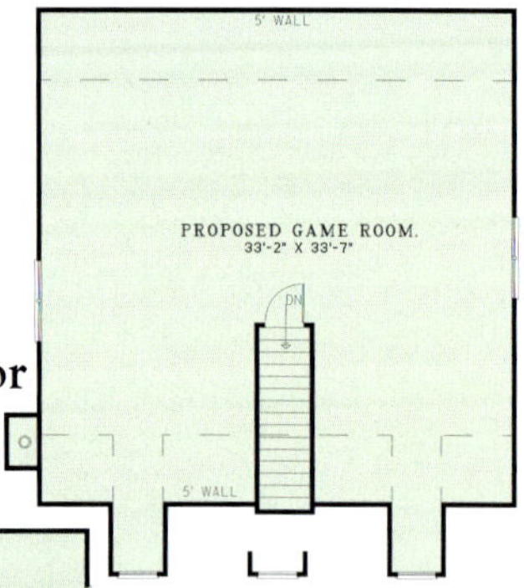

Bonus Floor

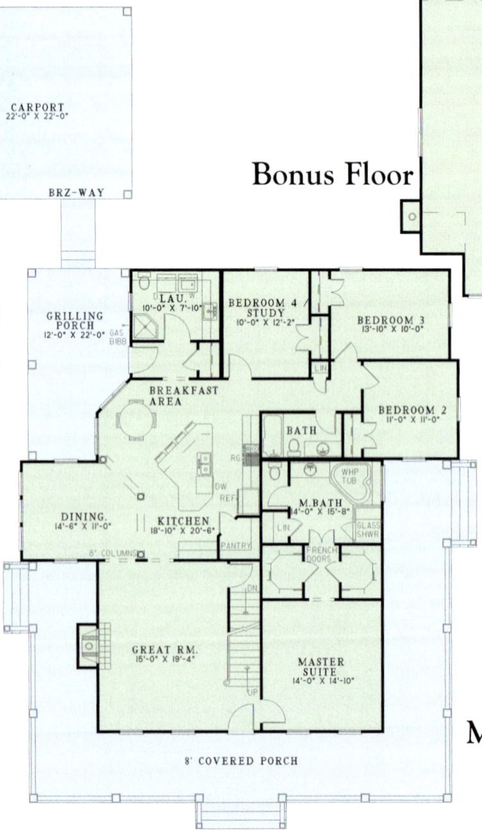

Main Floor

320 Olive Street

Width: 60' 6"
Depth: 91' 4"
Total Living: 2,039 sq. ft.*
*Bonus Floor: 1,155 sq. ft.
Main Ceiling: 9 ft.
Bonus Ceiling: 8 ft.
Bedrooms: 4
Baths: 3

Foundation: Crawl, Slab, Optional Basement, Optional Daylight Basement
Plan Options: page 93

Price Tier: C

Similar plans can be viewed and ordered at www.nelsondesigngroup.com

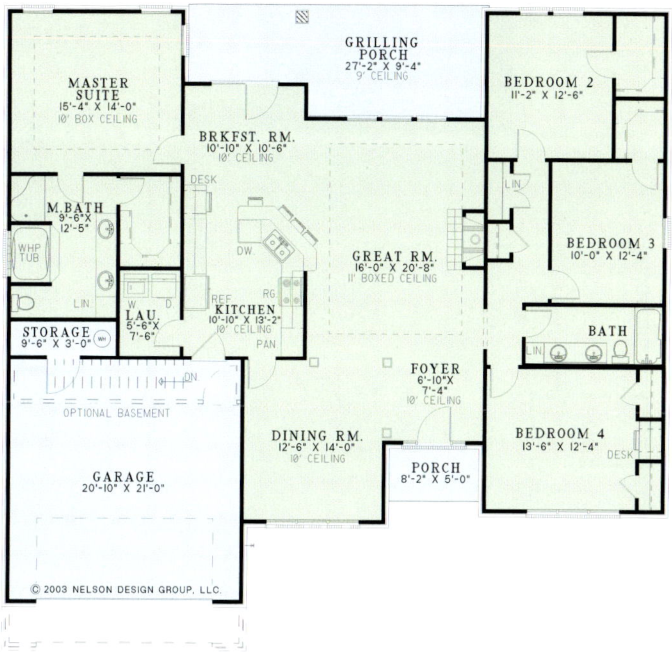

788 Spruce Street

Width: 59' 8"
Depth: 52' 0"
Total Living: 2,050 sq. ft.
Main Ceiling: 9 ft.
Bedrooms: 4
Baths: 2

Foundation: Crawl, Slab, Optional Basement, Optional Daylight Basement
Plan Options: page 93

Price Tier: C

Any plan can be modified to your specific needs - Call 1-800-590-2423 for pricing

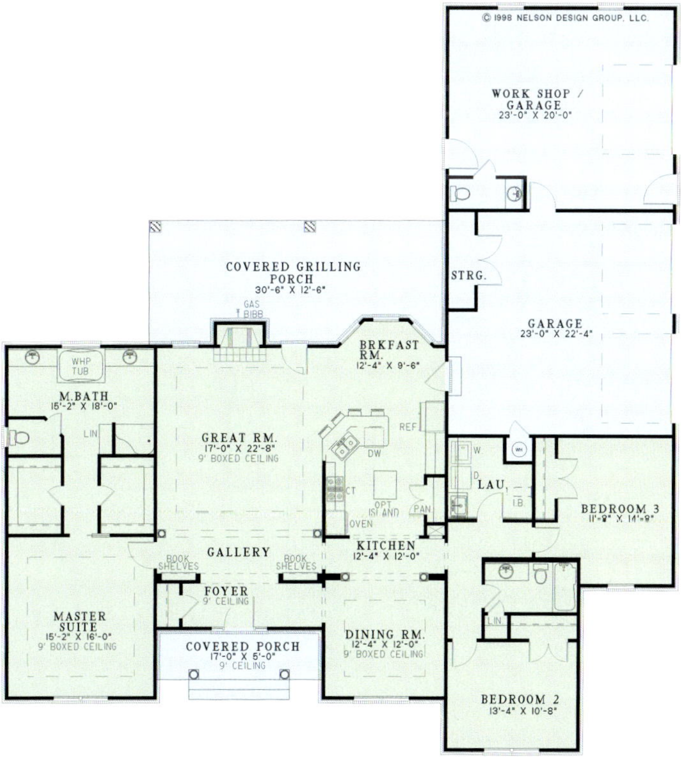

255 Cherry Street

Width: 69' 2"
Depth: 74' 10"
Total Living: 2,096 sq. ft.
Main Ceiling: 8 ft.
Bedrooms: 3
Baths: 2 1/2

Foundation: Crawl, Slab, Basement, Daylight Basement
Plan Options: page 93

Price Tier: C

190 Cherry Street

Width: 64' 8"
Depth: 62' 1"
Total Living: 2,107 sq. ft.
Main Ceiling: 8 ft.
Bedrooms: 4
Baths: 2 1/2

Foundation: Crawl, Slab, Basement, Daylight Basement
Plan Options: page 93

Price Tier: C

To order call toll free 1-800-590-2423

256 Olive Street

Width: 63' 10"
Depth: 72' 2"
Total Living: 2,131 sq. ft.
Main Ceiling: 9 ft.
Bedrooms: 3
Baths: 2 1/2

Foundation: Crawl, Slab, Optional Basement, Optional Daylight Basement
Plan Options: page 93

Price Tier: C

Similar plans can be viewed and ordered at www.nelsondesigngroup.com

194 *Hickory Place*

Width: 58' 6"
Depth: 64' 6"
Total Living: 2,133 sq. ft.
Main Ceiling: 9 ft.
Bedrooms: 3
Baths: 2

Foundation: Crawl, Slab, Basement, Daylight Basement
Plan Options: page 93

Price Tier: C

Any plan can be modified to your specific needs - Call 1-800-590-2423 for pricing

467 *Kensington Cove*

Width: 65' 2"
Depth: 63' 8"
Total Living: 2,147 sq. ft.
Main Ceiling: 8 ft.
Bedrooms: 4
Baths: 2 1/2

Foundation: Crawl, Slab, Optional Basement, Optional Daylight Basement
Plan Options: page 93

Price Tier: C

Bonus Floor

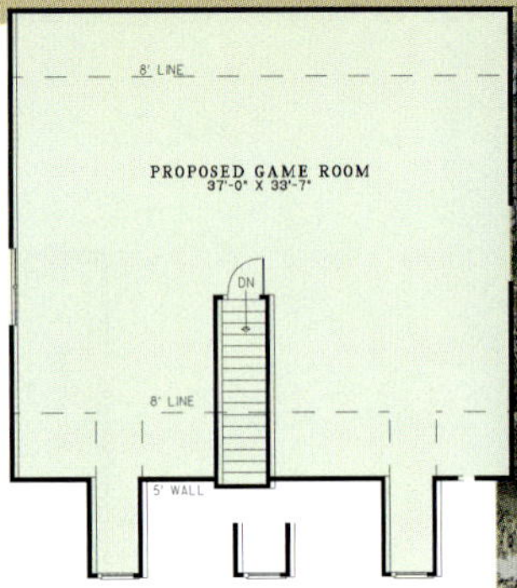

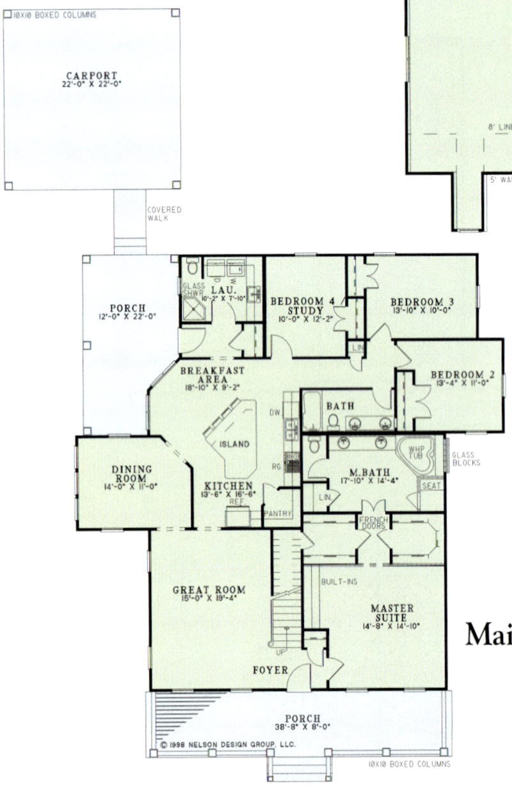

Main Floor

340 Olive Street

Width: 62' 10"
Depth: 91' 4"
Total Living: 2,186 sq. ft.*
*Bonus Floor: 1,283 sq. ft.
Main Ceiling: 9 ft.
Bonus Ceiling: 8 ft.
Bedrooms: 4
Baths: 3

Foundation: Crawl, Slab, Basement, Daylight Basement
Plan Options: page 93

Price Tier: C

To order call toll free 1-800-590-2423

202 Glendale Avenue

Width: 58' 0"
Depth: 69' 6"
Total Living: 2,189 sq. ft.
Main Ceiling: 9 ft.
Bedrooms: 4
Baths: 2

Foundation: Crawl, Slab, Optional Basement, Optional Daylight Basement
Plan Options: page 93

Price Tier: C

Similar plans can be viewed and ordered at www.nelsondesigngroup.com

From the Village at WINDSTONE III™

Bonus Floor

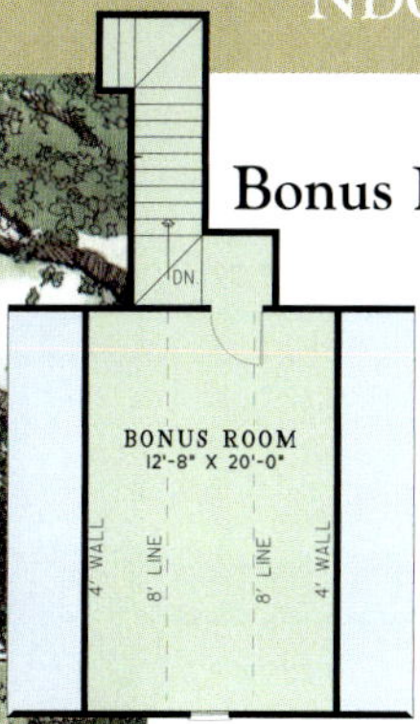

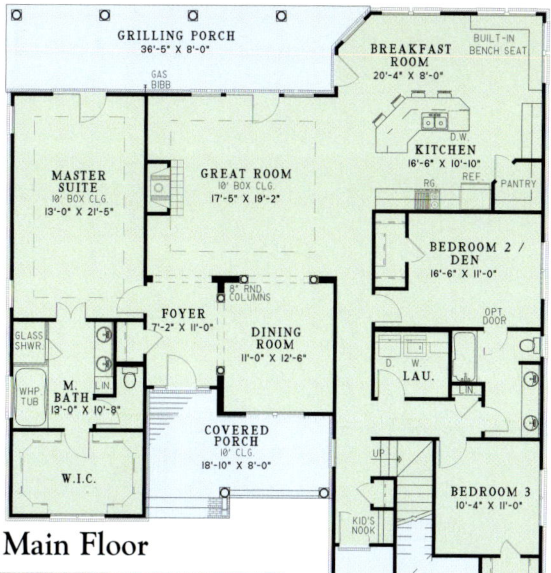

Main Floor

537 *Windstone Place*

Width: 54' 0"
Depth: 76' 10"
Total Living: 2,211 sq. ft.*
*Bonus Floor: 278 sq. ft.
Main Ceiling: 9 ft.
Bonus Ceiling: 8 ft.
Bedrooms: 3
Baths: 2

Foundation: Crawl, Slab, Optional Basement, Optional Daylight Basement
Plan Options: page 93

Price Tier: C

Any plan can be modified to your specific needs - Call 1-800-590-2423 for pricing

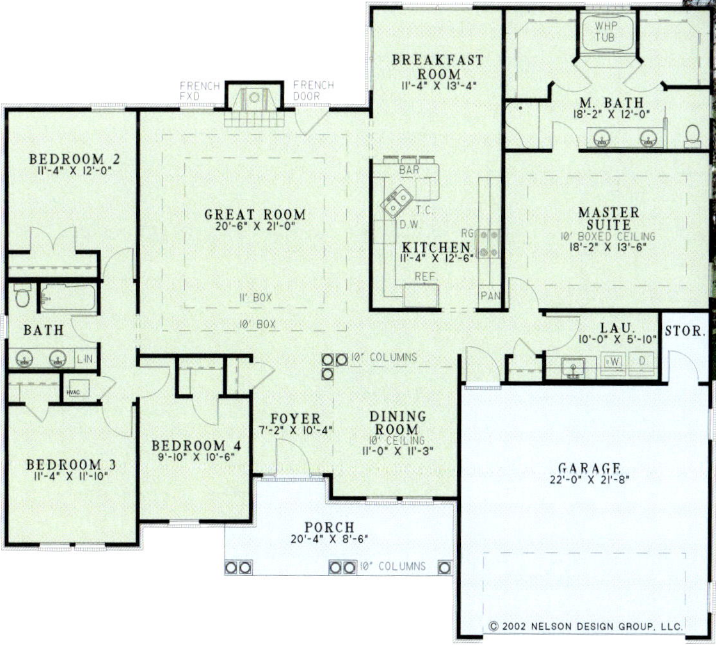

651 *Olive Street*

Width: 63' 0"
Depth: 54' 10"
Total Living: 2,214 sq. ft.
Main Ceiling: 9 ft.
Bedrooms: 4
Baths: 2

Foundation: Crawl, Slab, Optional Basement, Optional Daylight Basement
Plan Options: page 93

Price Tier: C

700 Linden Avenue

Width: 61' 2"
Depth: 55' 6"
Total Living: 2,217 sq. ft.
Main Ceiling: 9 ft.
Bedrooms: 4
Baths: 2

Foundation: Crawl, Slab, Optional Basement, Optional Daylight Basement
Plan Options: page 93

Price Tier: C

To order call toll free 1-800-590-2423

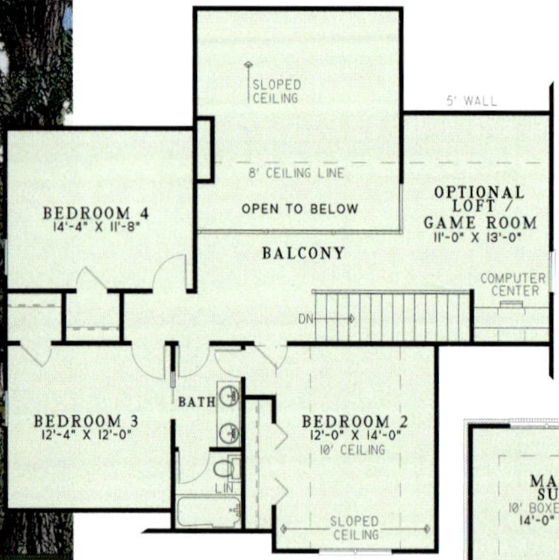

Upper Floor

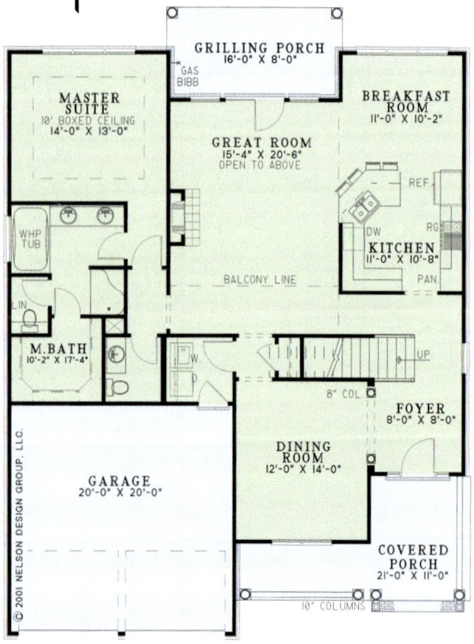

Main Floor

604 Cypress Drive

Width: 41' 8"
Depth: 55' 6"
Main Floor: 1,449 sq. ft.
Upper Floor: 795 sq. ft.
Total Living: 2,244 sq. ft.*
***Bonus:** 181 sq. ft.
Main Ceiling: 9 ft.
Upper Ceiling: 8 ft.

Bedrooms: 4
Baths: 2 1/2
Foundation: Crawl, Slab, Optional Basement, Optional Daylight Basement
Plan Options: page 93

Price Tier: C

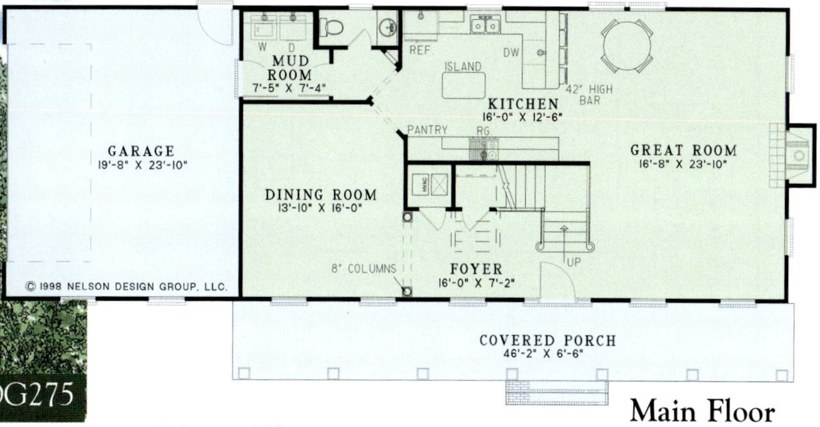

Main Floor

Upper Floor

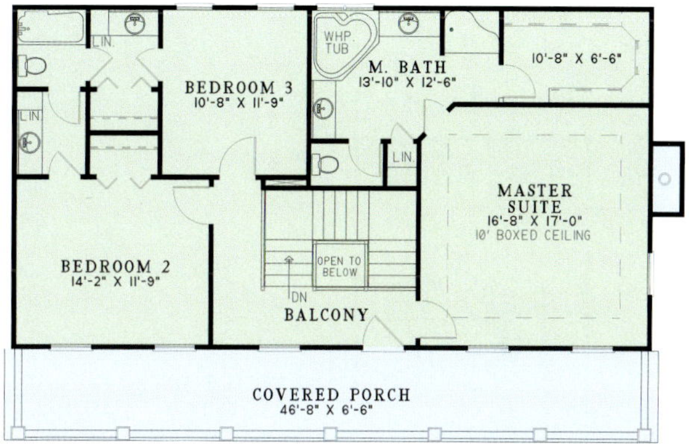

275 Olive Street

Width: 69' 6"
Depth: 31' 0"
Main Floor: 1,168 sq. ft.
Upper Floor: 1,100 sq. ft.
Total Living: 2,268 sq. ft.
Main Ceiling: 9 ft.
Upper Ceiling: 9 ft.

Bedrooms: 3
Baths: 2 1/2
Foundation: Crawl, Slab, Basement, Daylight Basement
Plan Options: page 93

Price Tier: C

Any plan can be modified to your specific needs - Call 1-800-590-2423 for pricing

Bonus Floor

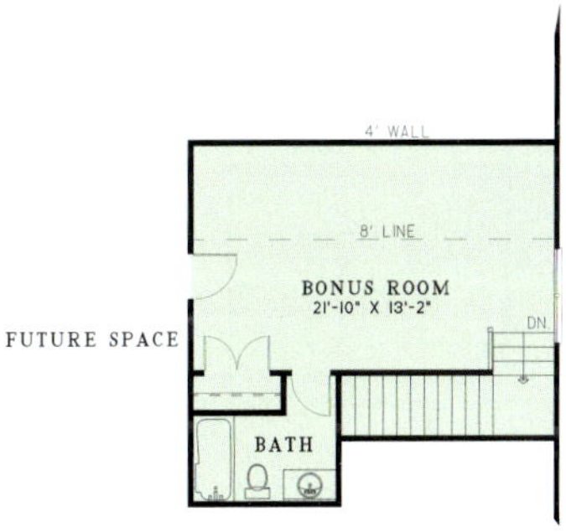

Main Floor

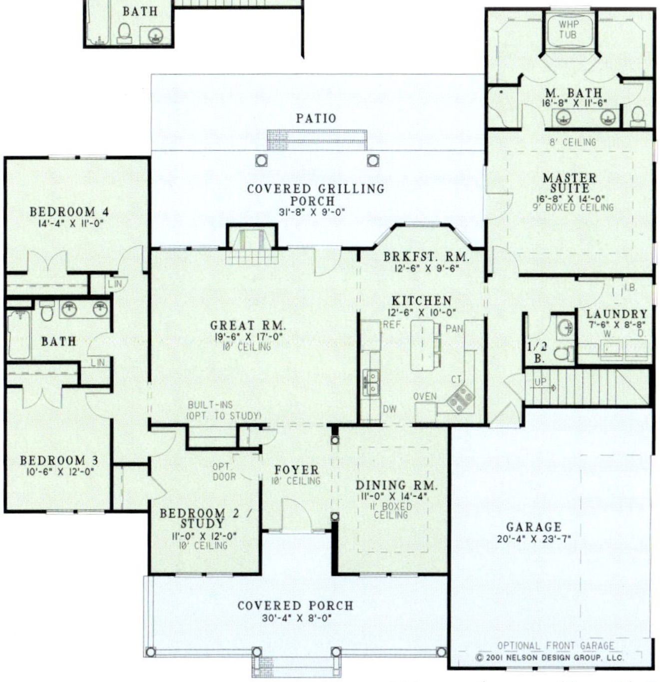

NDG526B Elevation

526 Olive Street

Width: 66' 0"
Depth: 65' 2"
Total Living: 2,261 sq. ft.*
*Bonus Floor: 367 sq. ft.
Main Ceiling: 9 ft.
Bonus Ceiling: 8 ft.

Bedrooms: 4
Baths: 2 1/2
Foundation: Crawl, Slab, Basement, Daylight Basement
Plan Options: page 93

Price Tier: C

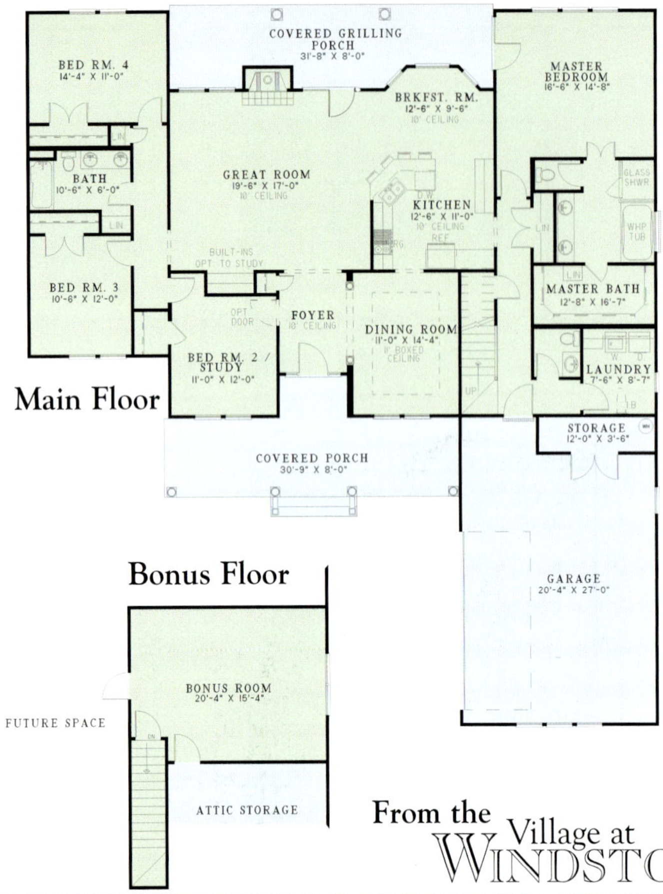

528 Windstone Place

Width: 66' 0"
Depth: 72' 7"
Total Living: 2,354 sq. ft.*
*Bonus Floor: 326 sq. ft.
Main Ceiling: 9 ft.
Bonus Ceiling: 8 ft.

Bedrooms: 4
Baths: 2 1/2
Foundation: Crawl, Slab, Optional Basement, Optional Daylight Basement
Plan Options: page 93

Price Tier: C

From the Village at WINDSTONE III™

To order call toll free 1-800-590-2423

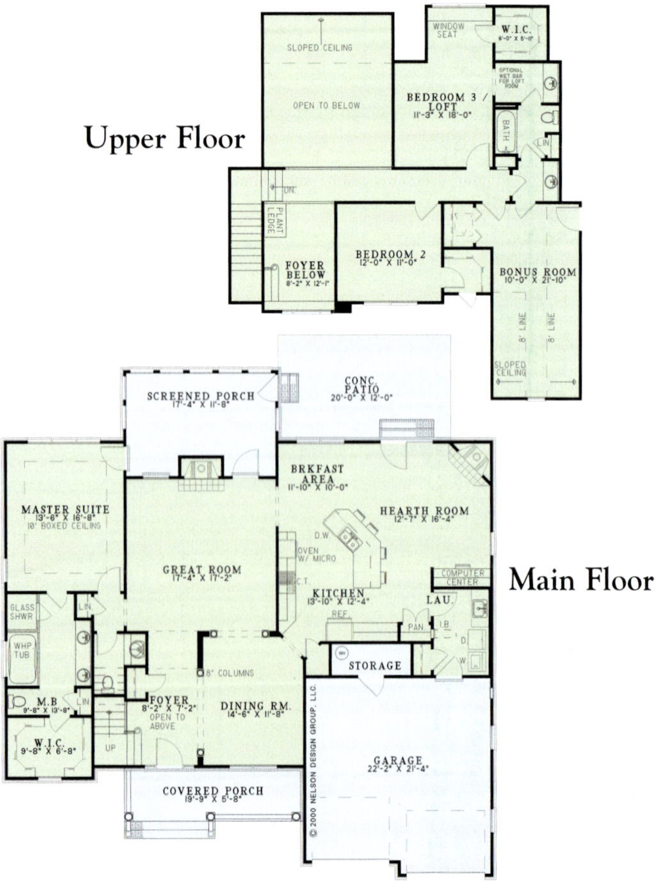

511 Magnolia Drive

Width: 56' 8"
Depth: 57' 4"
Main Floor: 1,776 sq. ft.
Upper Floor: 584 sq. ft.
Total Living: 2,360 sq. ft.*
*Bonus: 262 sq. ft.
Main Ceiling: 9 ft.
Upper Ceiling: 8 ft.

Bedrooms: 3
Baths: 2 1/2
Foundation: Crawl, Slab, Optional Basement, Optional Daylight Basement
Plan Options: page 93

Price Tier: C

Similar plans can be viewed and ordered at www.nelsondesigngroup.com

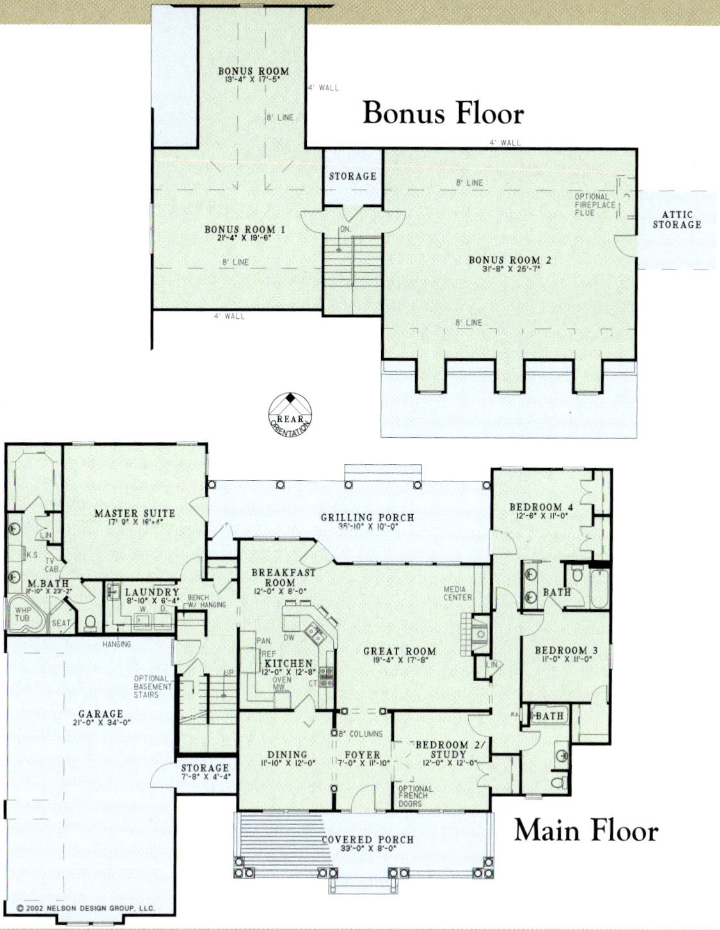

943 Quail Drive

Width: 76' 10"
Depth: 59' 2"
Total Living: 2,373 sq. ft.*
*Bonus 1: 687 sq. ft.
*Bonus 2: 896 sq. ft.
Main Ceiling: 9 ft.
Bonus Ceiling: 8 ft.

Bedrooms: 4
Baths: 3
Foundation: Crawl, Slab, Optional Basement, Optional Daylight Basement
Plan Options: page 93

Price Tier: C

Any plan can be modified to your specific needs - Call 1-800-590-2423 for pricing

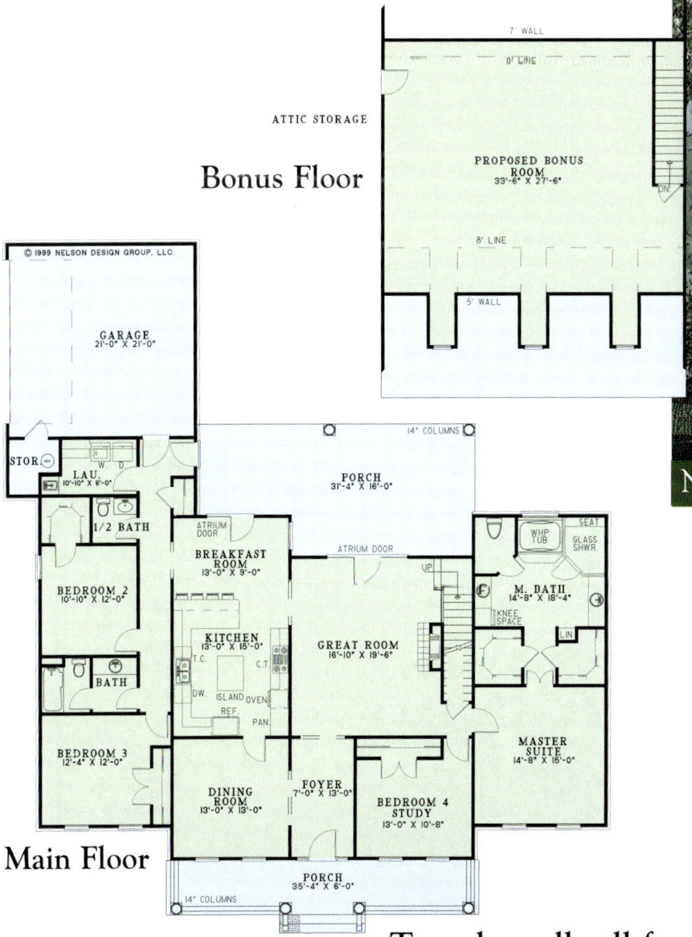

614 Country Lane

Width: 68' 0"
Depth: 74' 0"
Total Living: 2,388 sq. ft.*
*Bonus Floor: 974 sq. ft.
Main Ceiling: 9 ft.
Bonus Ceiling: 8 ft.
Bedrooms: 4
Baths: 2 1/2

Foundation: Crawl, Slab, Optional Basement, Optional Daylight Basement
Plan Options: page 93

Price Tier: C

Main Floor

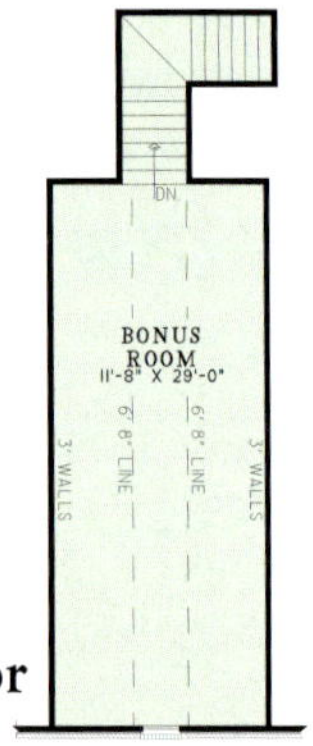

Bonus Floor

563 Country Club Drive

Width: 66' 4"
Depth: 67' 2"
Total Living: 2,405 sq. ft.*
*Bonus Floor: 358 sq. ft.
Main Ceiling: 9 ft.
Bonus Ceiling: 8 ft.
Bedrooms: 4
Baths: 3

Foundation: Crawl, Slab, Optional Basement, Optional Daylight Basement
Plan Options: page 93

Price Tier: C

To order call toll free 1-800-590-2423

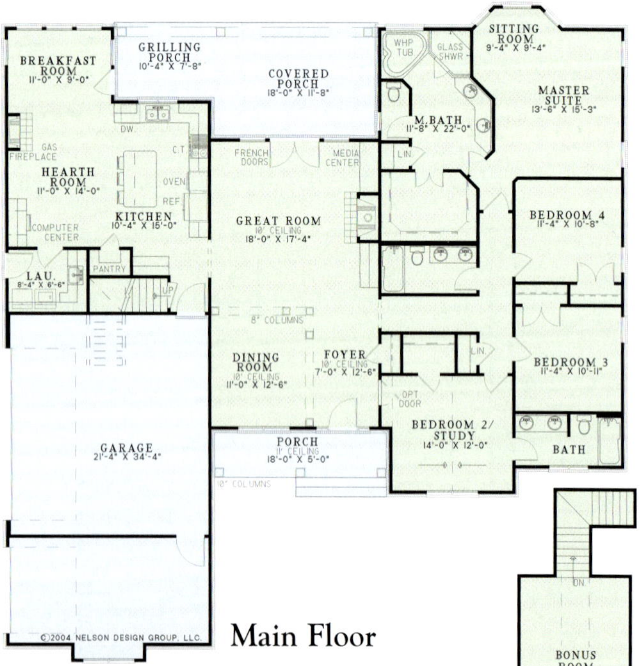

Main Floor

942 Magnolia Drive

Width: 66' 4"
Depth: 68' 10"
Total Living: 2,405 sq. ft.*
*Bonus Floor: 358 sq. ft.
Main Ceiling: 9 ft.
Bonus Ceiling: 8 ft.
Bedrooms: 4
Baths: 3

Foundation: Crawl, Slab, Optional Basement, Optional Daylight Basement
Plan Options: page 93

Price Tier: C

NDG942 Alternate View

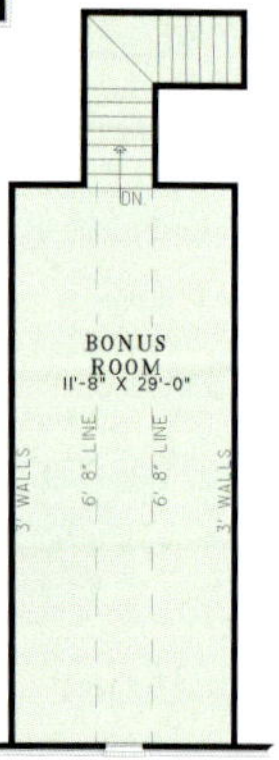

Bonus Floor

Similar plans can be viewed and ordered at www.nelsondesigngroup.com

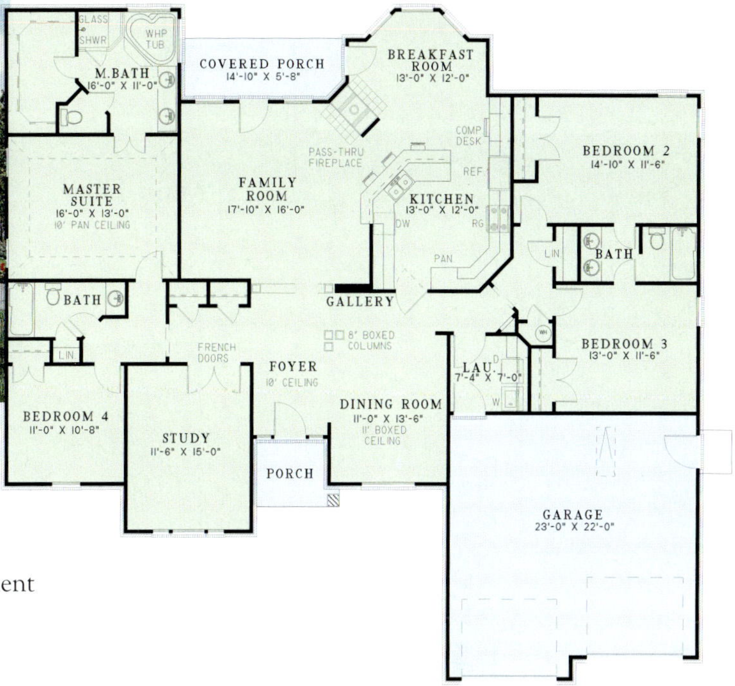

204 Richmond Drive

Width: 65' 8"
Depth: 61' 7"
Total Living: 2,439 sq. ft.
Main Ceiling: 9 ft.
Bedrooms: 4
Baths: 3

Foundation: Crawl, Slab, Basement, Daylight Basement
Plan Options: page 93

Price Tier: C

Any plan can be modified to your specific needs - Call 1-800-590-2423 for pricing

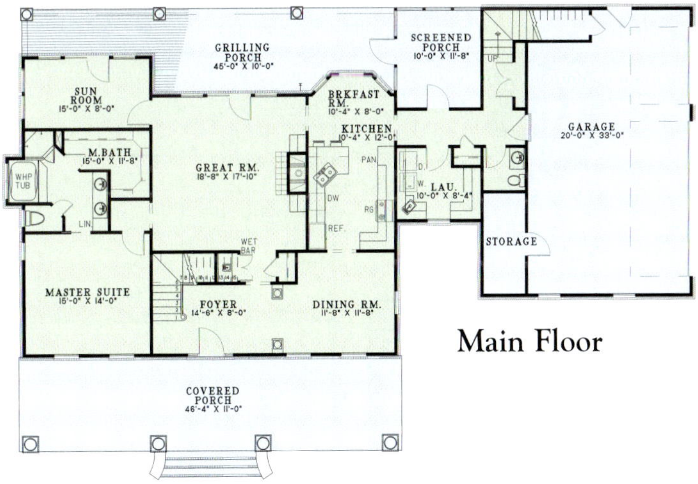

Main Floor

Upper Floor

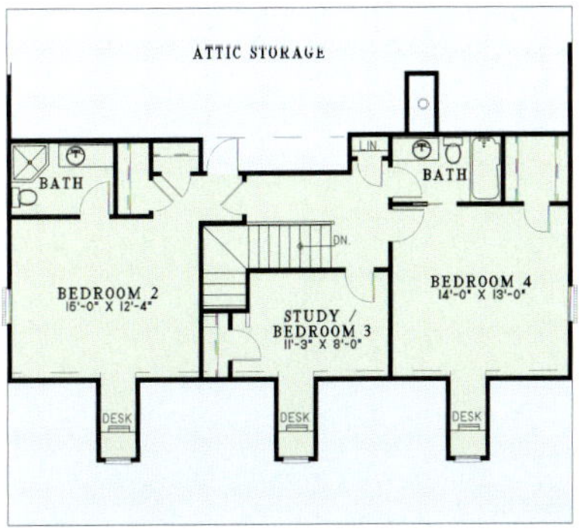

Bonus

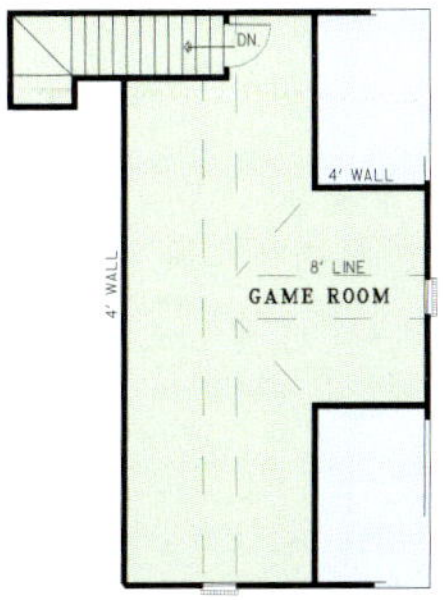

377 Olive Street

Width: 82' 10"
Depth: 51' 6"
Main Floor: 1,674 sq. ft.
Upper Floor: 802 sq. ft.
Total Living: 2,476 sq. ft.*
*Bonus: 460 sq. ft.
Main Ceiling: 9 ft.
Upper Ceiling: 8 ft.

Bedrooms: 4
Baths: 3 1/2
Foundation: Crawl, Slab, Optional Basement, Optional Daylight Basement
Plan Options: page 93

Price Tier: C

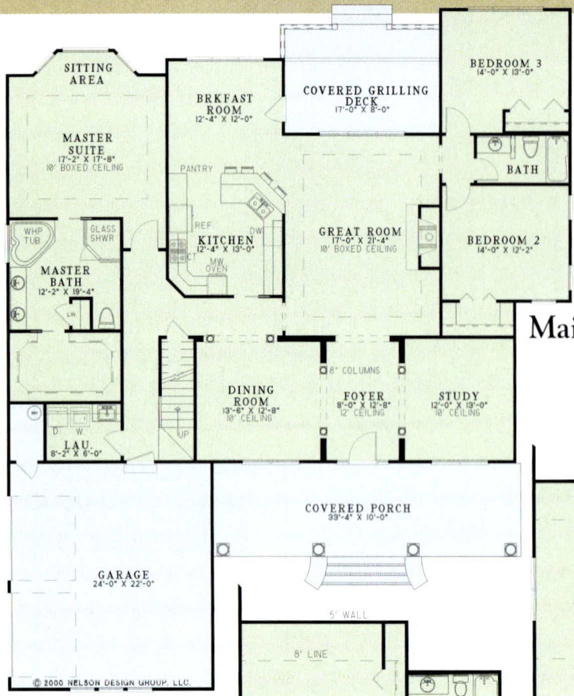

Main Floor

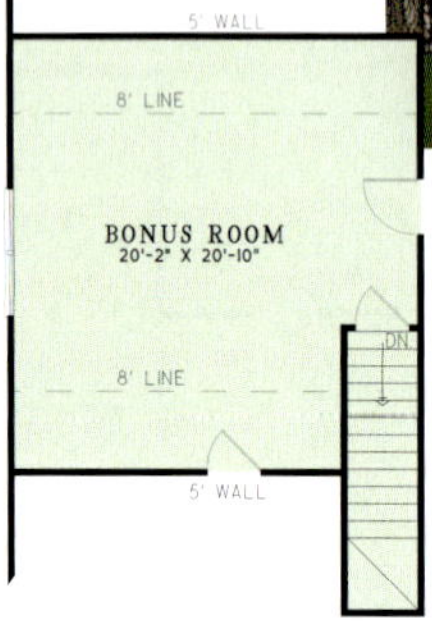

Bonus Floor B

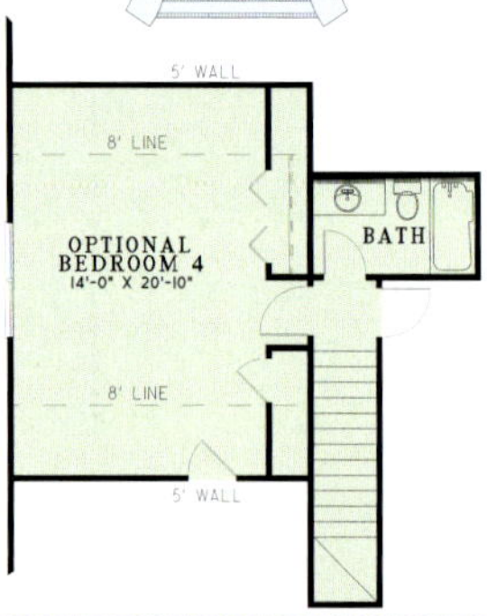

Bonus Floor A

541 Timber Drive

Width: 62' 2"
Depth: 73' 0"
Total Living: 2,499 sq. ft.*
*Bonus Floor A: 421 sq. ft.
*Bonus Floor B: 438 sq. ft.
Main Ceiling: 9 ft.
Bonus Ceiling: 8 ft.

Bedrooms: 3
Baths: 2
Foundation: Crawl, Slab, Optional Basement, Optional Daylight Basement
Plan Options: page 93

Price Tier: C

To order call toll free 1-800-590-2423

From the

Midtown ESTATE COLLECTION™

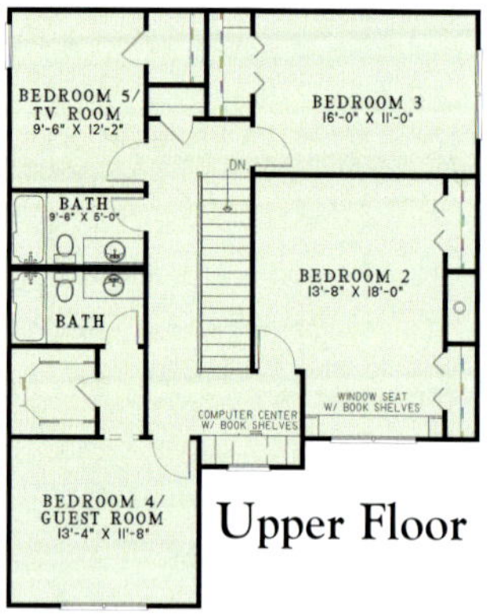

Upper Floor

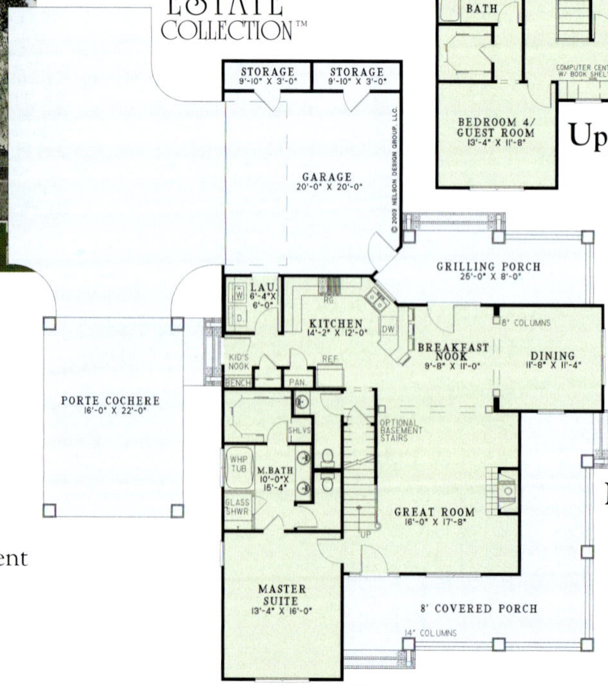

Main Floor

918 Summer Avenue

Width: 64' 0"
Depth: 68' 6"
Main Floor: 1,360 sq. ft.
Upper Floor: 1,156 sq. ft.
Total Living: 2,516 sq. ft.
Main Ceiling: 9 ft.
Upper Ceiling: 8 ft.

Bedrooms: 5
Baths: 3 1/2
Foundation: Crawl, Slab, Optional Basement, Optional Daylight Basement
Plan Options: page 93

Price Tier: D

Similar plans can be viewed and ordered at www.nelsondesigngroup.com

184 *Kensington Cove*

Width: 63' 4"
Depth: 59' 10"
Total Living: 2,525 sq. ft.
Main Ceiling: 9 ft.
Bedrooms: 3
Baths: 2 1/2

Foundation: Crawl, Slab, Basement, Daylight Basement
Plan Options: page 93

Price Tier: D

Any plan can be modified to your specific needs - Call 1-800-590-2423 for pricing

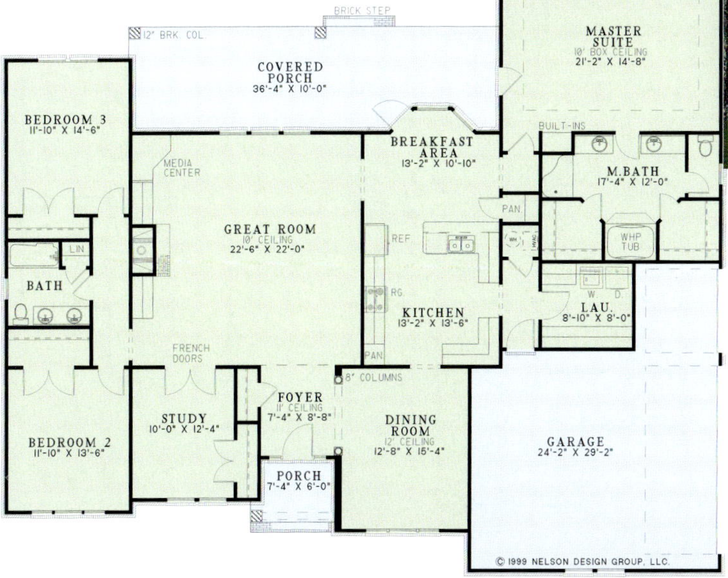

371 *Dogwood Avenue*

Width: 70' 4"
Depth: 57' 2"
Total Living: 2,534 sq. ft.
Main Ceiling: 9 ft.
Bedrooms: 3
Baths: 2

Foundation: Crawl, Slab, Optional Basement, Optional Daylight Basement
Plan Options: page 93

Price Tier: D

Bonus Floor

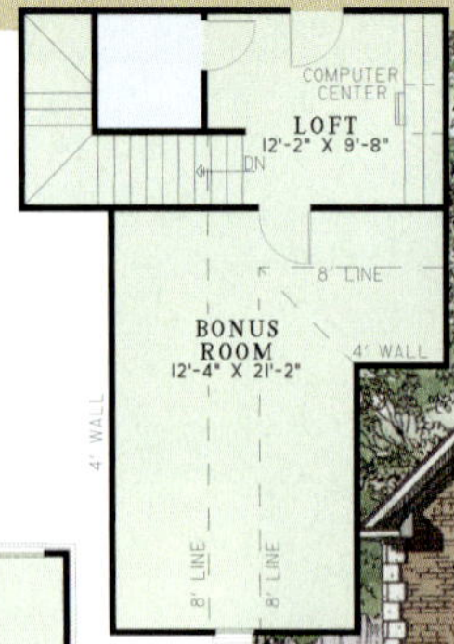

Main Floor

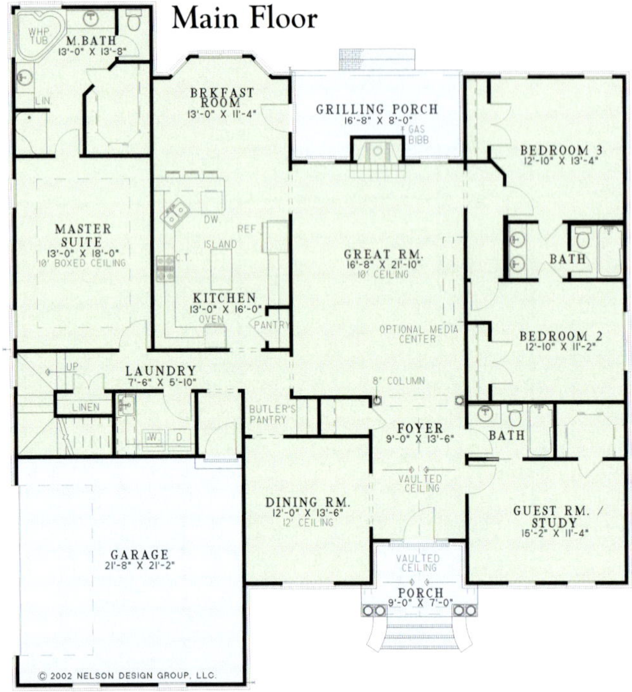

664 Dogwood Lane

Width: 59' 6"
Depth: 64' 2"
Total Living: 2,542 sq. ft.*
*Bonus Floor: 473 sq. ft.
Main Ceiling: 9 ft.
Bonus Ceiling: 8 ft.
Bedrooms: 4
Baths: 3

Foundation: Crawl, Slab, Optional Basement, Optional Daylight Basement
Plan Options: page 93

Price Tier: D

To order call toll free 1-800-590-2423

539 Madison Drive

Width: 74' 7"
Depth: 70' 6"
Total Living: 2,556 sq. ft.
Main Ceiling: 9 ft.
Bedrooms: 4
Baths: 3

Foundation: Crawl, Slab
Plan Options: page 93

Price Tier: D

Similar plans can be viewed and ordered at www.nelsondesigngroup.com

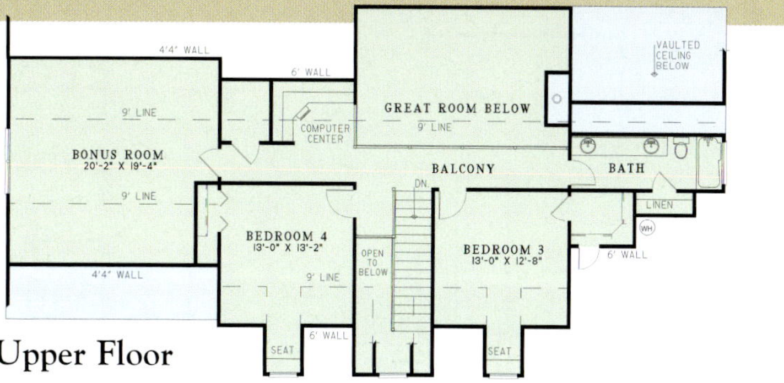

Upper Floor

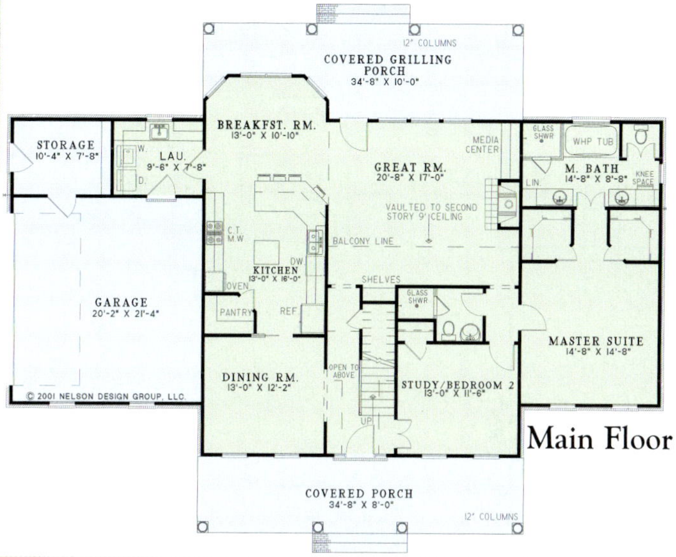

Main Floor

597 Hampton Circle

Width: 70' 2"
Depth: 53' 4"
Main Floor: 1,813 sq. ft.
Upper Floor: 790 sq. ft.
Total Living: 2,603 sq. ft.*
*Bonus: 410 sq. ft.
Main Ceiling: 9 ft.
Upper Ceiling: 9 ft.

Bedrooms: 4
Baths: 2 1/2
Foundation: Crawl, Slab, Optional Basement, Optional Daylight Basement
Plan Options: page 93

Price Tier: D

Any plan can be modified to your specific needs - Call 1-800-590-2423 for pricing

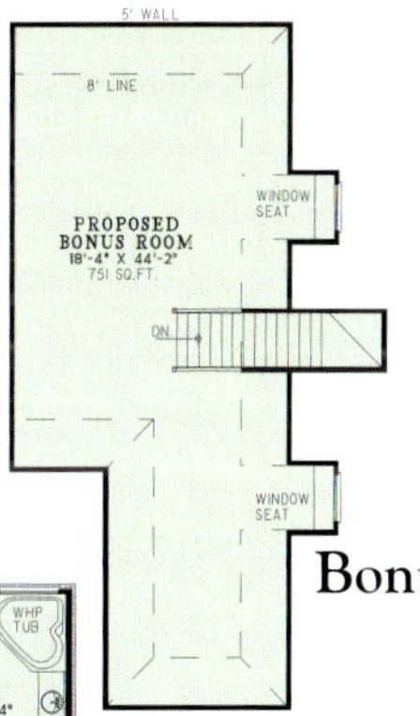

Bonus Floor

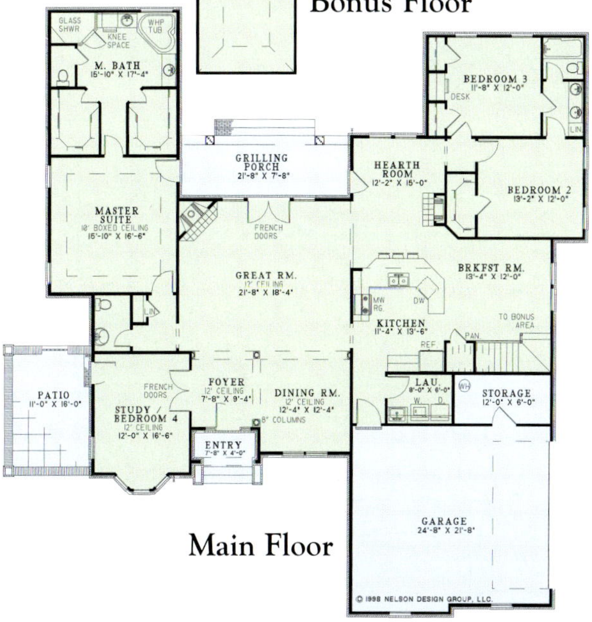

Main Floor

380 Cherry Street

Width: 67' 6"
Depth: 73' 10"
Total Living: 2,606 sq. ft.*
*Bonus Floor: 751 sq. ft.
Main Ceiling: 9 ft.
Bonus Ceiling: 8 ft.
Bedrooms: 4
Baths: 2 1/2

Foundation: Crawl, Slab, Basement, Daylight Basement
Plan Options: page 93

Price Tier: D

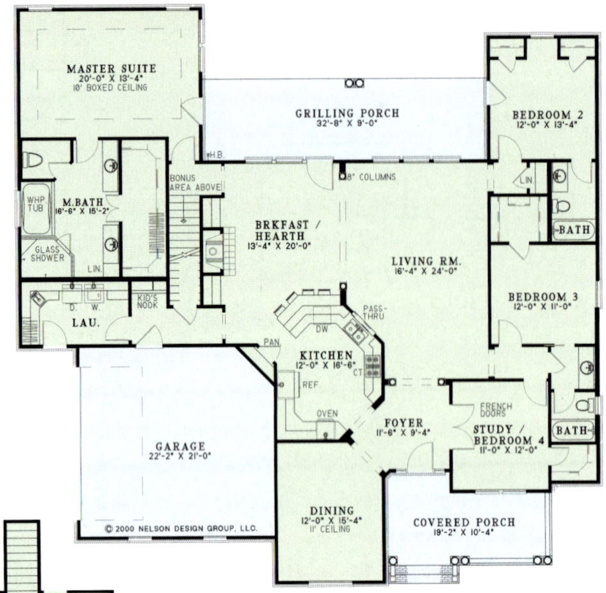

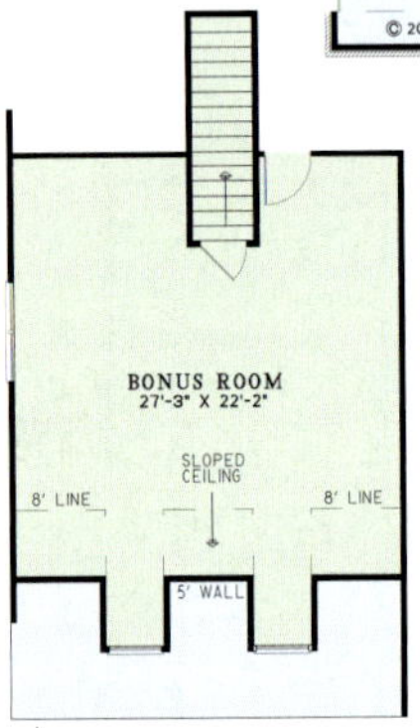

Main Floor

Bonus Floor

502 Willow Lane

Width: 66' 4"
Depth: 64' 0"
Total Living: 2,624 sq. ft.*
*Bonus Floor: 561 sq. ft.
Main Ceiling: 9 ft.
Bonus Ceiling: 8 ft.
Bedrooms: 4
Baths: 3

Foundation: Crawl, Slab, Optional Basement, Optional Daylight Basement
Plan Options: page 93

Price Tier: D

To order call toll free 1-800-590-2423

Upper Floor

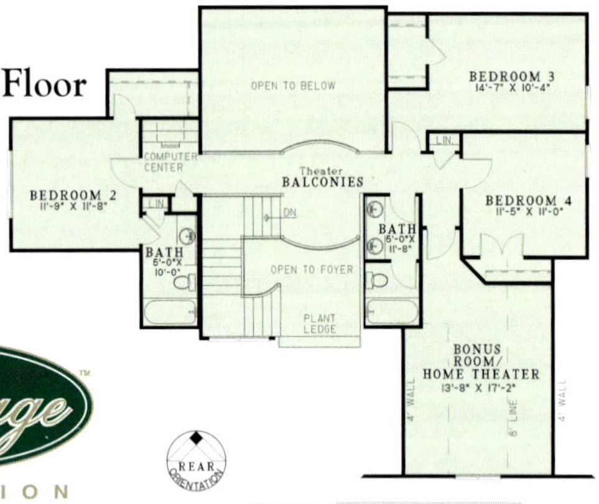

From the Heritage NDG Since 1985 Collection

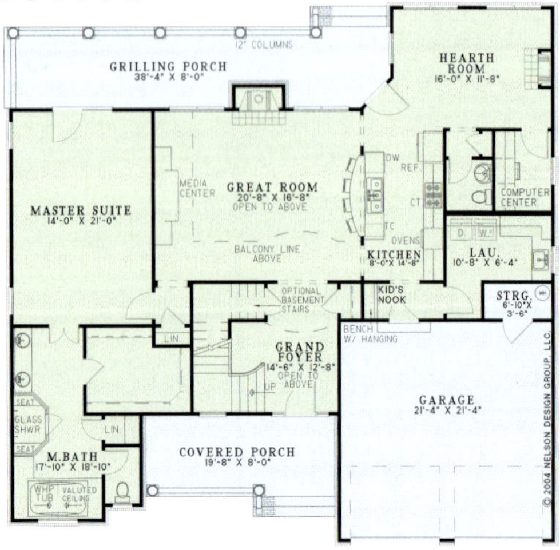

Main Floor

951 Ambrose Boulevard

Width: 55' 0"
Depth: 52' 10"
Main Floor: 1,747 sq. ft.
Upper Floor: 895 sq. ft.
Total Living: 2,642 sq. ft.*
*Bonus: 263 sq. ft.
Main Ceiling: 9 ft.
Upper Ceiling: 8 ft.

Bedrooms: 4
Baths: 3 1/2
Foundation: Crawl, Slab, Optional Basement, Optional Daylight Basement
Plan Options: page 93

Price Tier: D

Similar plans can be viewed and ordered at www.nelsondesigngroup.com

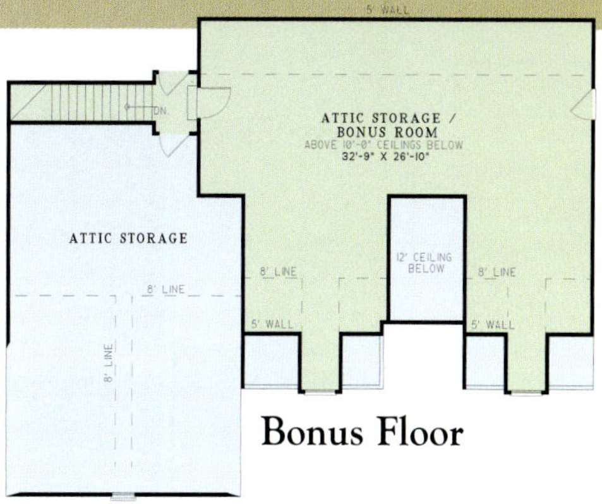

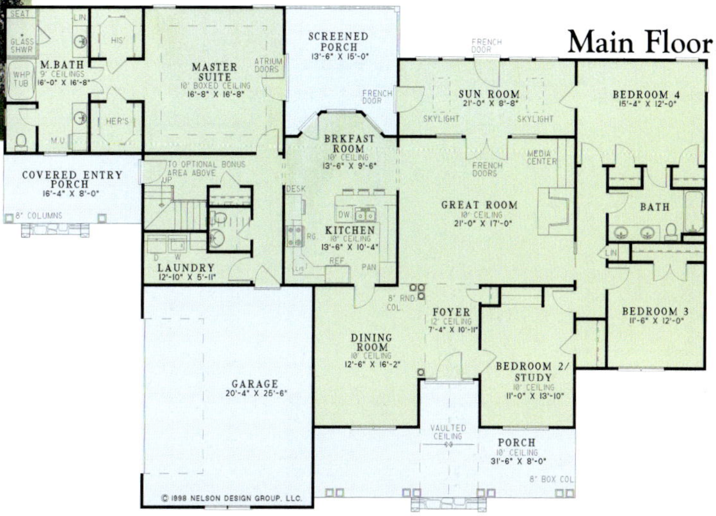

327 Willow Lane

Width: 84' 6"
Depth: 58' 6"
Total Living: 2,742 sq. ft.*
*Bonus Floor: 916 sq. ft.
Main Ceiling: 9 ft.
Bonus Ceiling: 8 ft.
Bedrooms: 4
Baths: 2 1/2

Foundation: Crawl, Slab
Basement,
Daylight Basement
Plan Options: page 93

Price Tier: D

Any plan can be modified to your specific needs - Call 1-800-590-2423 for pricing

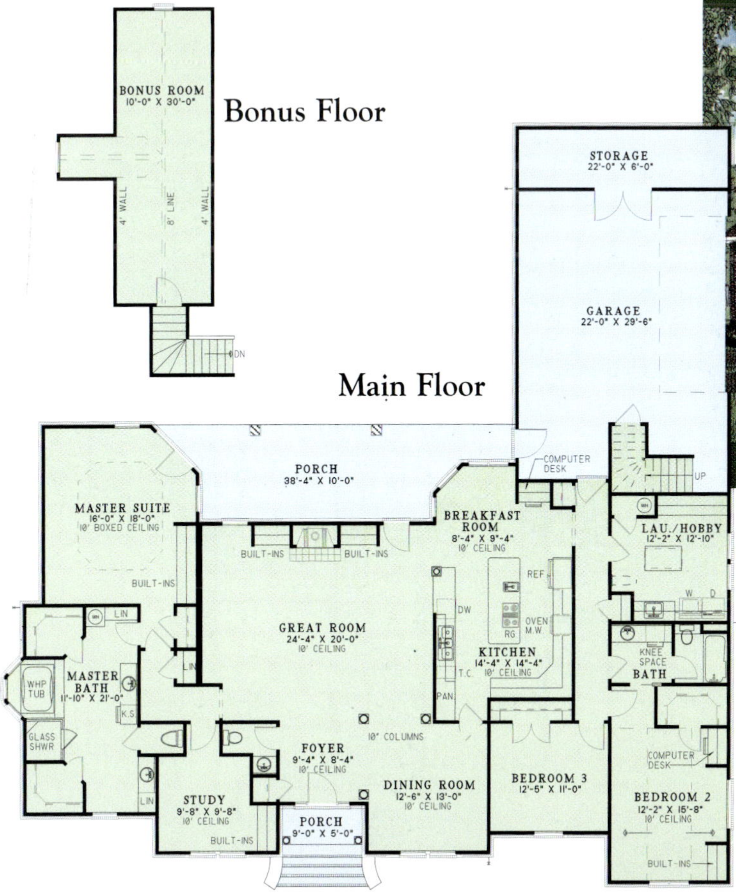

372 Richmond Cove

Width: 76' 8"
Depth: 77' 7"
Total Living: 2,742 sq. ft.*
*Bonus Floor: 352 sq. ft.
Main Ceiling: 9 ft.
Bonus Ceiling: 8 ft.

Bedrooms: 3
Baths: 2 1/2
Foundation: Crawl, Slab
Plan Options: page 93

Price Tier: D

Upper Floor

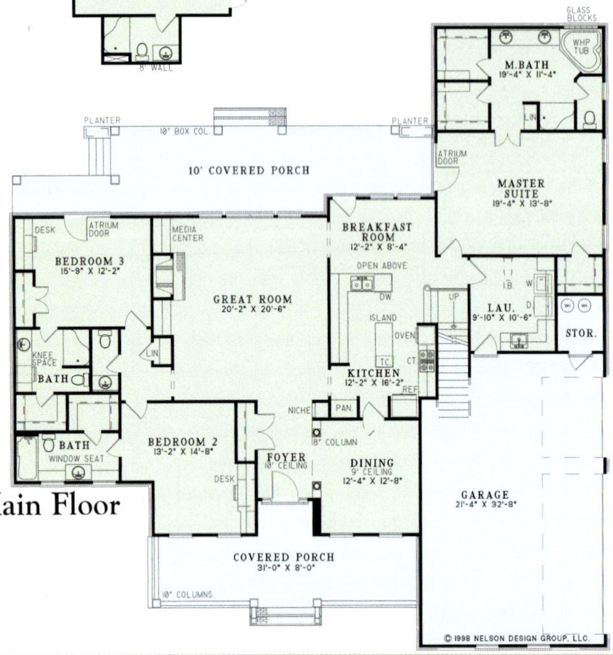

Main Floor

209 Olive Street

Width: 69' 0"
Depth: 69' 10"
Main Floor: 2,406 sq. ft.
Upper Floor: 349 sq. ft.
Total Living: 2,755 sq. ft.
Main Ceiling: 9 ft.
Upper Ceiling: 8 ft.

Bedrooms: 4
Baths: 3 1/2
Foundation: Crawl, Slab, Basement, Daylight Basement
Plan Options: page 93

Price Tier: D

To order call toll free 1-800-590-2423

Upper Floor

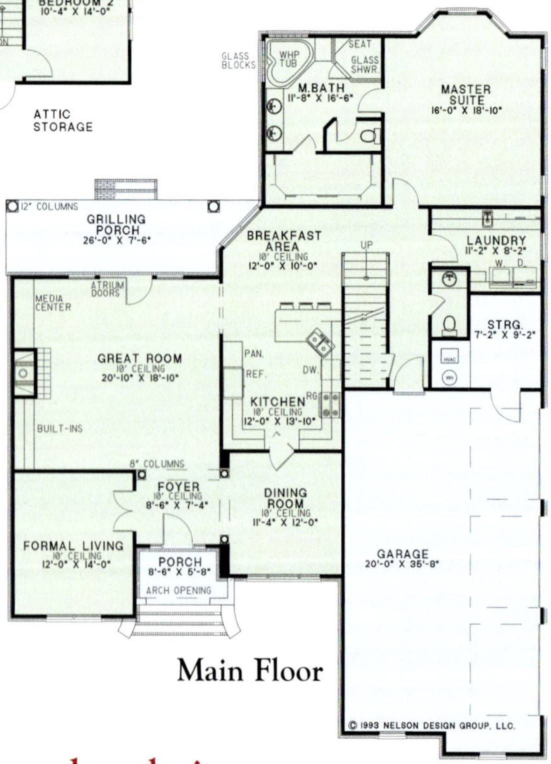

Main Floor

348 Willow Lane

Width: 54' 2"
Depth: 73' 6"
Main Floor: 1,895 sq. ft.
Upper Floor: 889 sq. ft.
Total Living: 2,784 sq. ft.
Main Ceiling: 9 ft.
Upper Ceiling: 9 ft.

Bedrooms: 4
Baths: 2 1/2
Foundation: Crawl, Slab, Basement, Daylight Basement
Plan Options: page 93

Price Tier: D

Similar plans can be viewed and ordered at www.nelsondesigngroup.com

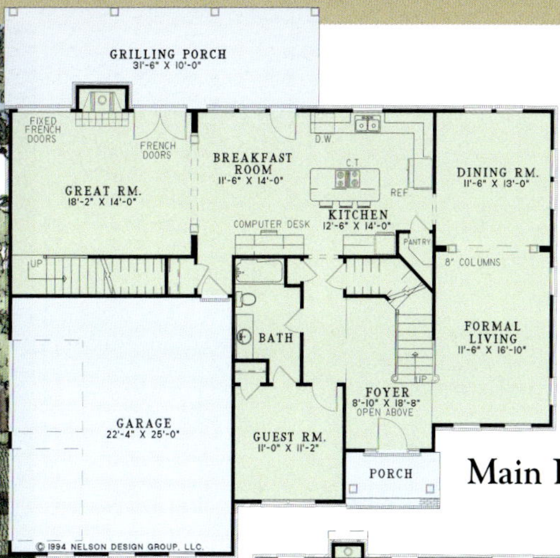

Main Floor

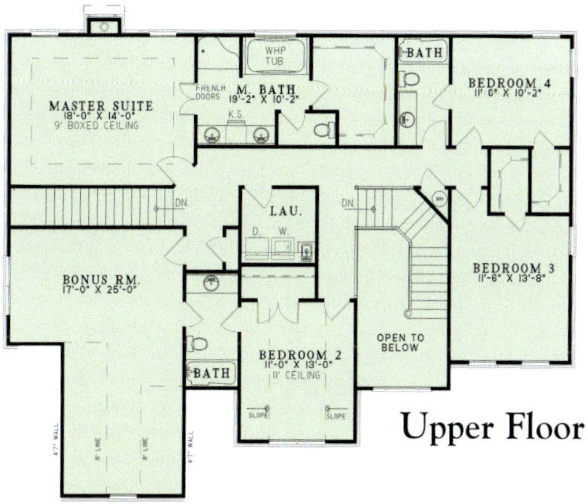

Upper Floor

164 Brittany Lane

Width: 55' 4"
Depth: 53' 10"
Main Floor: 1,547 sq. ft.
Upper Floor: 1,395 sq. ft.
Total Living: 2,942 sq. ft.*
*Bonus: 366 sq. ft.
Main Ceiling: 9 ft.
Upper Ceiling: 8 ft.

Bedrooms: 5
Baths: 4
Foundation: Crawl, Slab, Optional Basement, Optional Daylight Basement
Plan Options: page 93

Price Tier: D

Any plan can be modified to your specific needs - Call 1-800-590-2423 for pricing

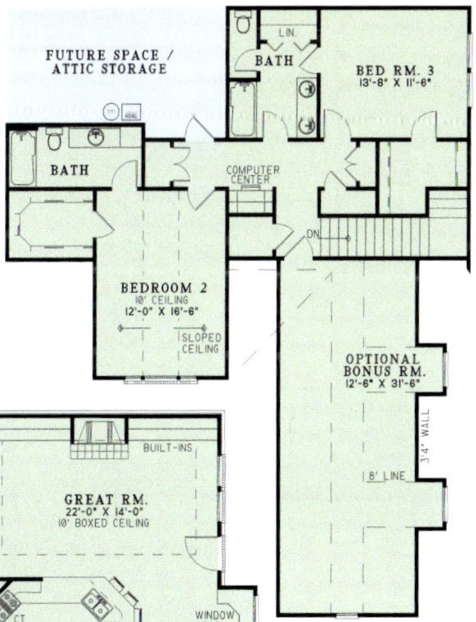

Upper Floor

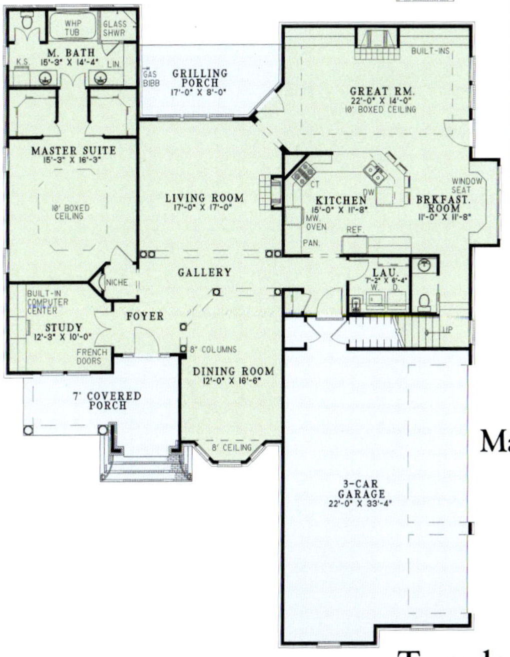

Main Floor

434 Dogwood Avenue

Width: 59' 0"
Depth: 73' 0"
Main Floor: 2,126 sq. ft.
Upper Floor: 823 sq. ft.
Total Living: 2,949 sq. ft.*
*Bonus: 442 sq. ft.
Main Ceiling: 9 ft.
Upper Ceiling: 8 ft.

Bedrooms: 3
Baths: 3 1/2
Foundation: Crawl, Slab, Optional Basement, Optional Daylight Basement
Plan Options: page 93

Price Tier: D

345 Sunset Drive

Width: 73' 6"
Depth: 80' 6"
Total Living: 2,951 sq. ft.
Main Ceiling: 9 ft.
Bedrooms: 4
Baths: 3

Foundation: Crawl, Slab, Basement, Daylight Basement
Plan Options: page 93

Price Tier: D

To order call toll free 1-800-590-2423

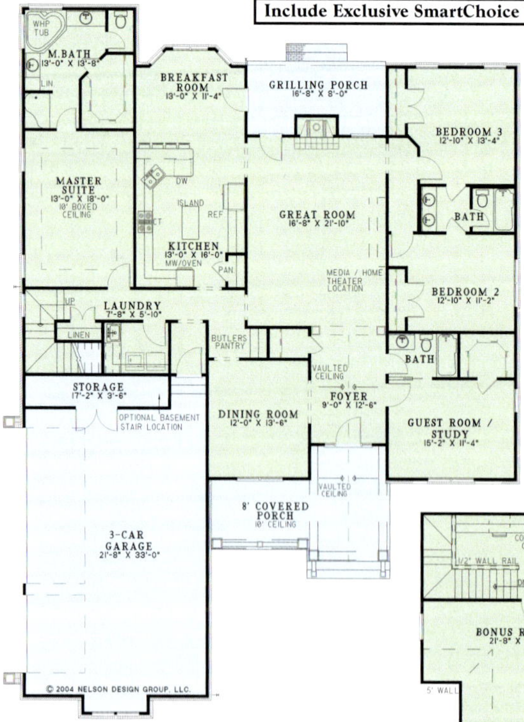

Main Floor

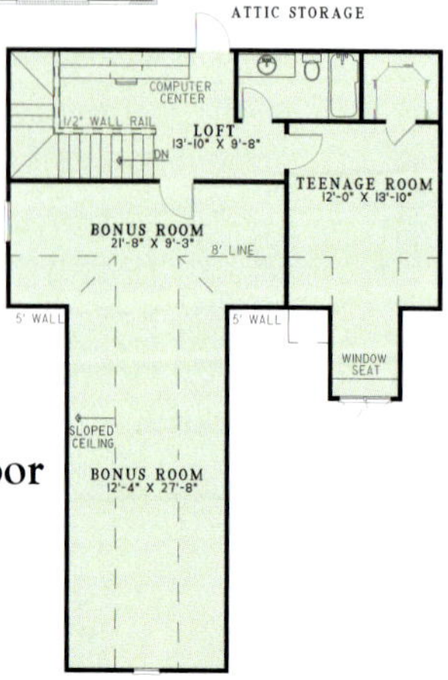

Upper Floor

946 Thomas Road

Width: 59' 6"
Depth: 81' 10"
Main Floor: 2,530 sq. ft.
Upper Floor: 445 sq. ft.
Total Living: 2,975 sq. ft.*
***Bonus:** 568 sq. ft.
Main Ceiling: 9 ft.
Upper Ceiling: 8 ft.

Bedrooms: 4
Baths: 4
Foundation: Crawl, Slab, Optional Basement, Optional Daylight Basement
Plan Options: page 93

Price Tier: D

Similar plans can be viewed and ordered at www.nelsondesigngroup.com

Upper Floor

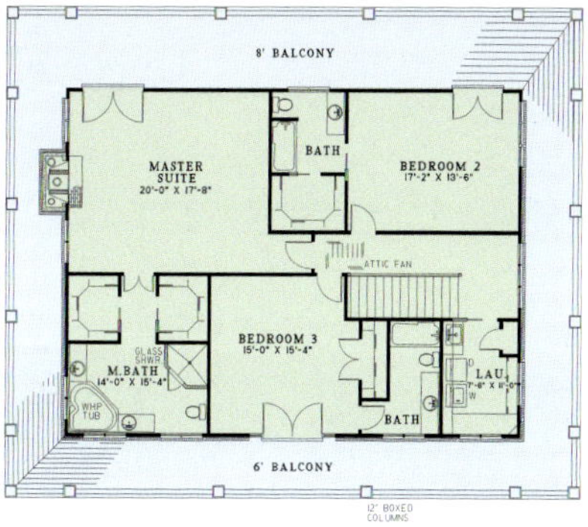

Main Floor

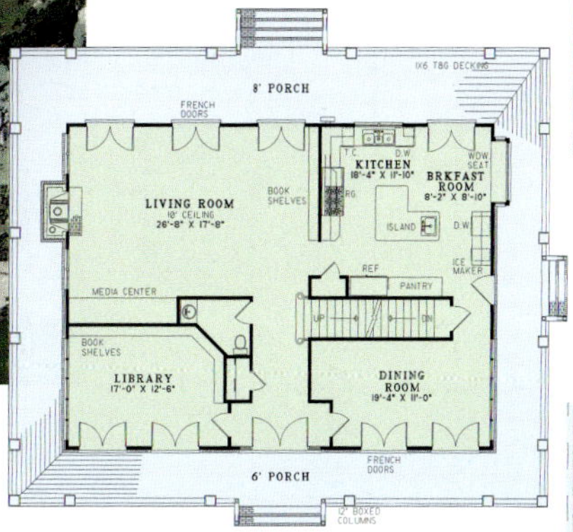

369 Waterfront Cove

Width: 58' 0"
Depth: 48' 0"
Main Floor: 1,564 sq. ft.
Upper Floor: 1,496 sq. ft.
Total Living: 3,060 sq. ft.
Main Ceiling: 10 ft.
Upper Ceiling: 9 ft.

Bedrooms: 3
Baths: 3 full, 2 half
Foundation: Crawl, Slab, Basement, Daylight Basement
Plan Options: page 93

Price Tier: E

Lower Floor

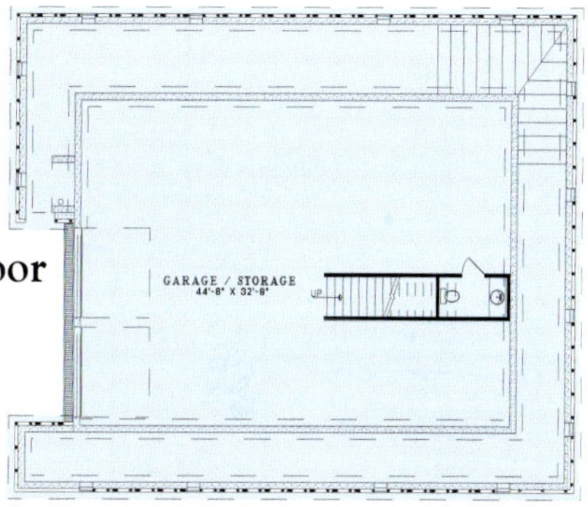

From The Waterfront Collection™

Any plan can be modified to your specific needs - Call 1-800-590-2423 for pricing

Main Floor

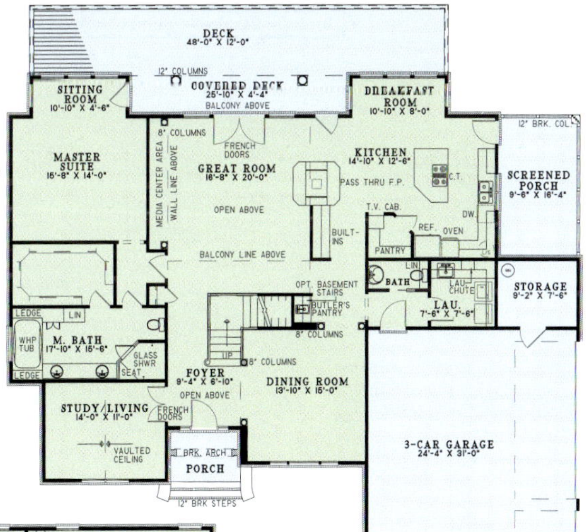

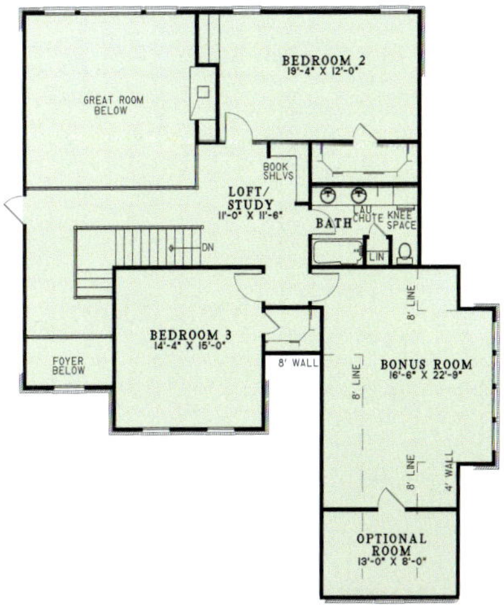

Upper Floor

362 Cherry Street

Width: 66' 8"
Depth: 60' 4"
Main Floor: 2,107 sq. ft.
Upper Floor: 1,001 sq. ft.
Total Living: 3,108 sq. ft.*
*Bonus: 485 sq. ft.
Main Ceiling: 9 ft.
Upper Ceiling: 8 ft.

Bedrooms: 3
Baths: 2 1/2
Foundation: Crawl, Slab, Optional Basement, Optional Daylight Basement
Plan Options: page 93

Price Tier: E

Upper Floor

Main Floor

631 Cherry Street

Width: 65' 0"
Depth: 89' 11"
Main Floor: 2,802 sq. ft.
Upper Floor: 890 sq. ft.
Total Living: 3,692 sq. ft.*
*Bonus: 439 sq. ft.
Main Ceiling: 10 ft.
Upper Ceiling: 9 ft.

Bedrooms: 5
Baths: 5
Foundation: Crawl, Slab, Optional Basement, Optional Daylight Basement
Plan Options: page 93

Price Tier: F

To order call toll free 1-800-590-2423

Upper Floor

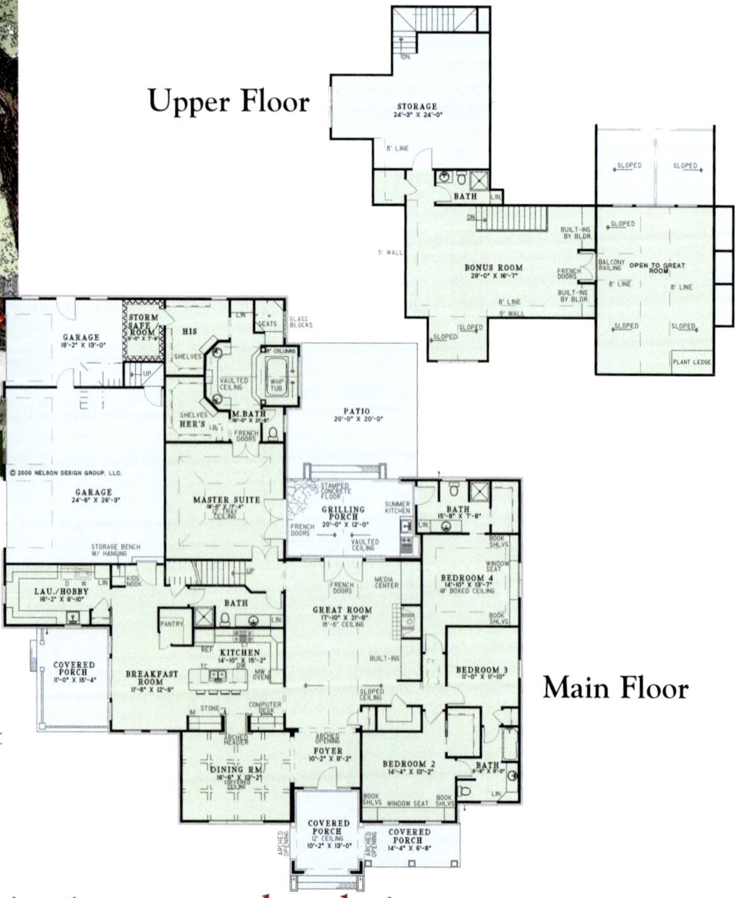

Main Floor

501 Brittany Lane

Width: 79' 10"
Depth: 86' 8"
Main Floor: 3,354 sq. ft.
Upper Floor: 615 sq. ft.
Total Living: 3,969 sq. ft.
Main Ceiling: 9 ft.
Upper Ceiling: 9 ft.

Bedrooms: 4
Baths: 4
Foundation: Crawl, Slab, Optional Basement, Optional Daylight Basement
Plan Options: page 93

Price Tier: F

Similar plans can be viewed and ordered at www.nelsondesigngroup.com

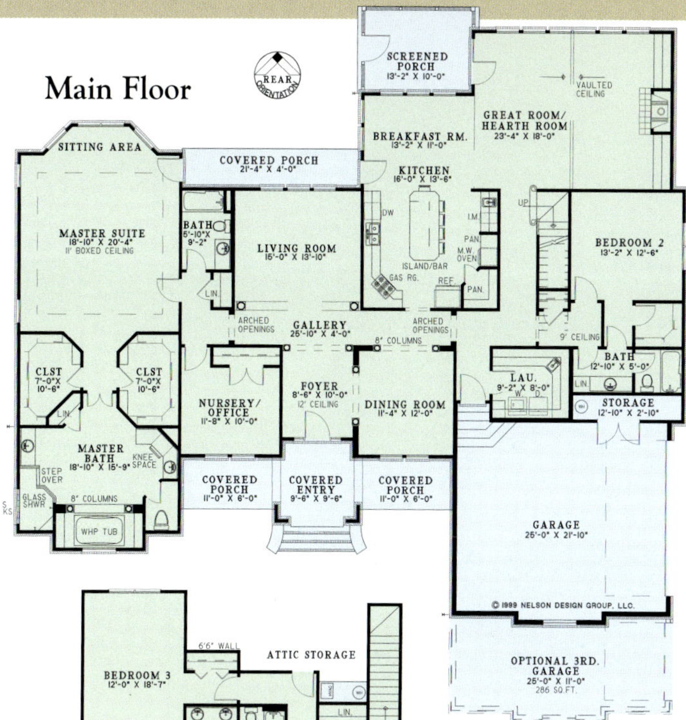

304 Cherry Street

Width: 79' 6"
Depth: 71' 4"
Main Floor: 3,185 sq. ft.
Upper Floor: 716 sq. ft.
Total Living: 3,901 sq. ft.
Main Ceiling: 10 ft.
Upper Ceiling: 8 ft.

Bedrooms: 3
Baths: 4
Foundation: Crawl, Slab, Optional Basement, Optional Daylight Basement
Plan Options: page 93

Price Tier: F

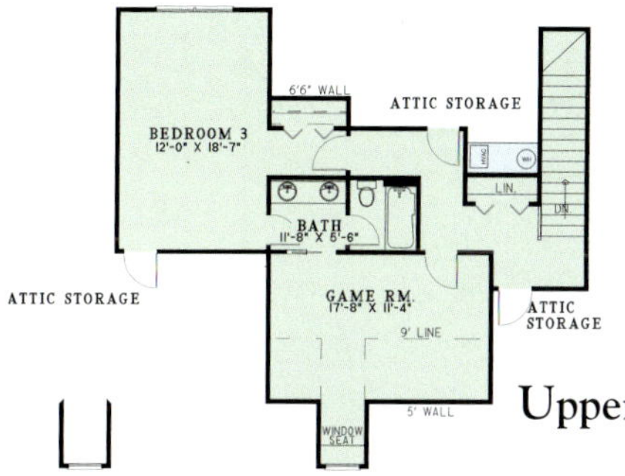

Any plan can be modified to your specific needs - Call 1-800-590-2423 for pricing

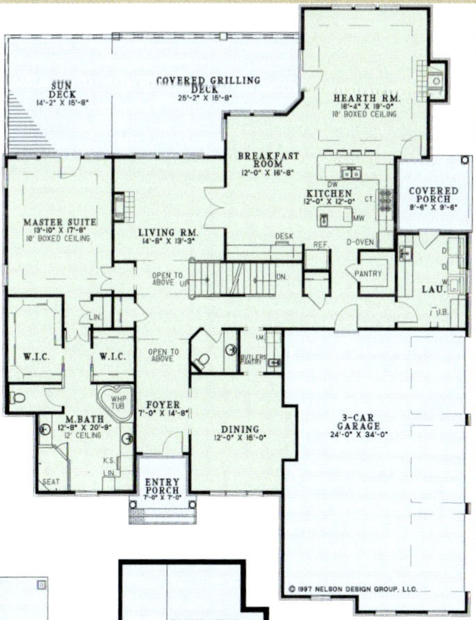

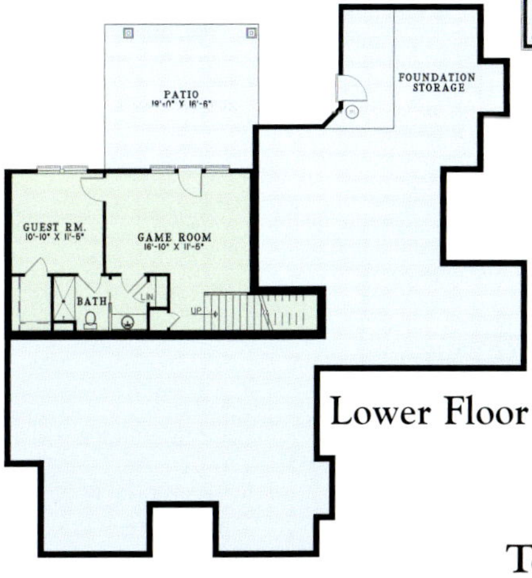

258 Cherry Street

Width: 61' 6"
Depth: 78' 6"
Main Floor: 2,405 sq. ft.
Upper Floor: 1,071 sq. ft.
Lower Floor: 546 sq. ft.
Total Living: 4,022 sq. ft.
Main Ceiling: 9 ft.

Upper Ceiling: 9 ft.
Lower Ceiling: 9 ft.
Bedrooms: 5
Baths: 4 1/2
Foundation: Daylight Basement
Plan Options: page 93

Price Tier: G

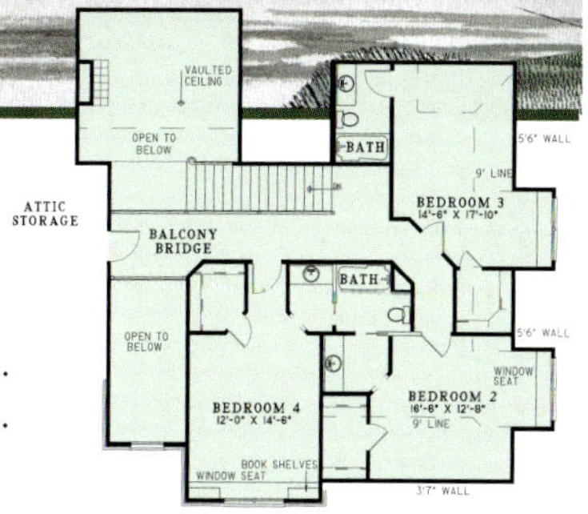

Upper Floor

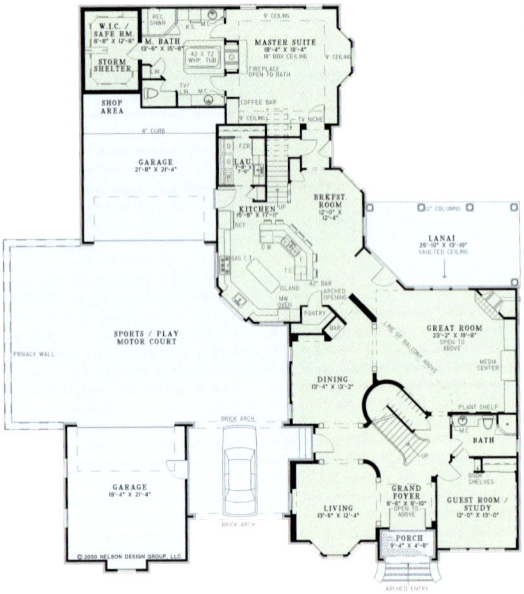

Main Floor

632 Cherry Street

Width: 85' 0"
Depth: 90' 6"
Main Floor: 2,958 sq. ft.
Upper Floor: 1,376 sq. ft.
Total Living: 4,334 sq. ft.*
*Bonus: 723 sq. ft.
Main Ceiling: 10 ft.
Upper Ceiling: 9 ft.

Bedrooms: 4
Baths: 4
Foundation: Crawl, Slab, Optional Basement, Optional Daylight Basement
Plan Options: page 93

Price Tier: G

To order call toll free 1-800-590-2423

Main Floor

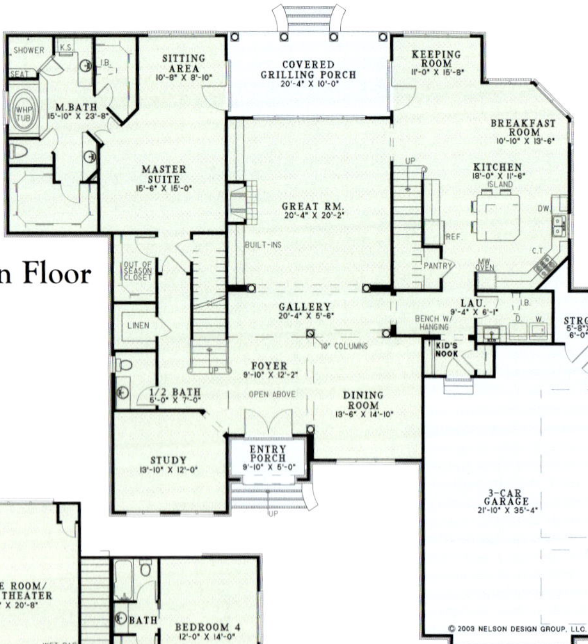

671 Dogwood Avenue

Width: 74' 4"
Depth: 74' 8"
Main Floor: 2,836 sq. ft.
Upper Floor: 1,524 sq. ft.
Total Living: 4,360 sq. ft.
Main Ceiling: 10 ft.
Upper Ceiling: 9 ft.

Bedrooms: 4
Baths: 3 full, 2 half
Foundation: Crawl, Slab, Optional Basement, Optional Daylight Basement
Plan Options: page 93

Price Tier: G

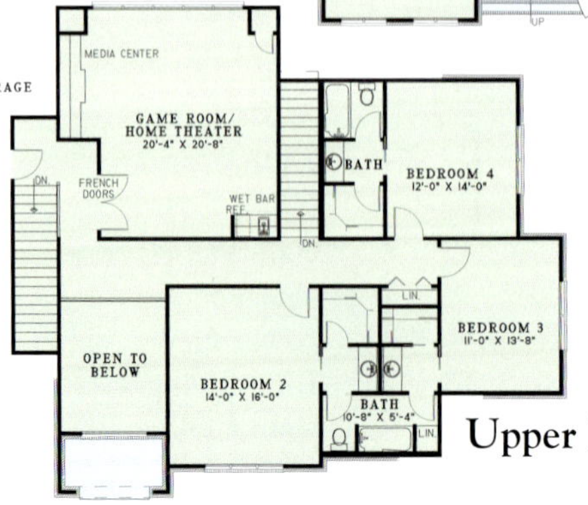

Upper Floor

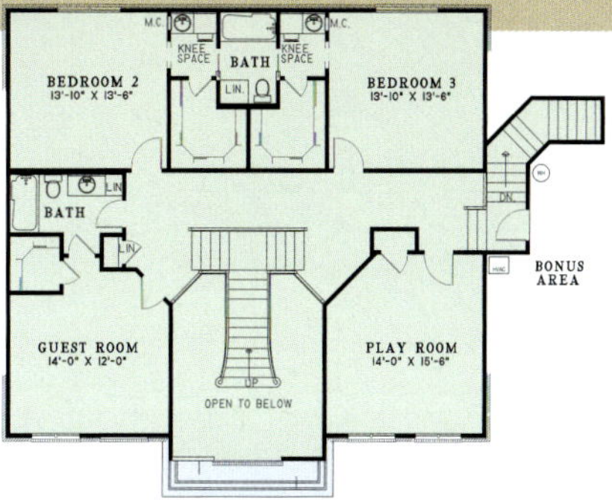

Upper Floor

Main Floor

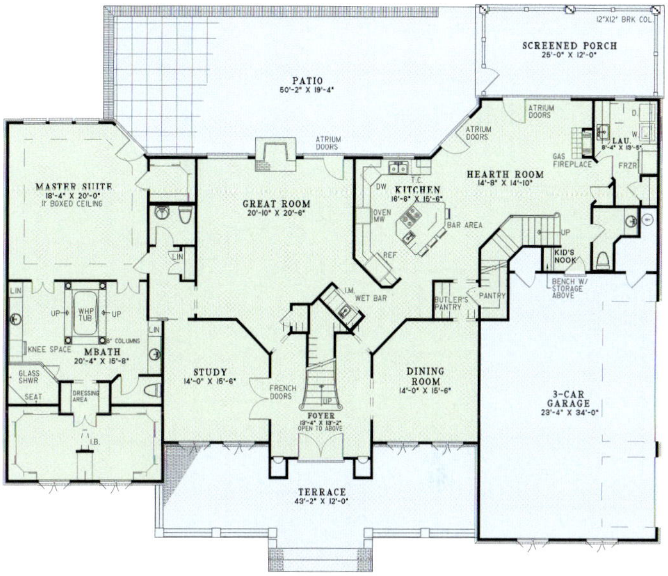

253 Birchwood Lane

Width: 87' 0"
Depth: 70' 0"
Main Floor: 3,086 sq. ft.
Upper Floor: 1,360 sq. ft.
Total Living: 4,446 sq. ft.
Main Ceiling: 10 ft.
Upper Ceiling: 9 ft.

Bedrooms: 4
Baths: 3 full, 2 half
Foundation: Crawl, Slab, Optional Basement, Optional Daylight Basement
Plan Options: page 93

Price Tier: G

Any plan can be modified to your specific needs - Call 1-800-590-2423 for pricing

Main Floor

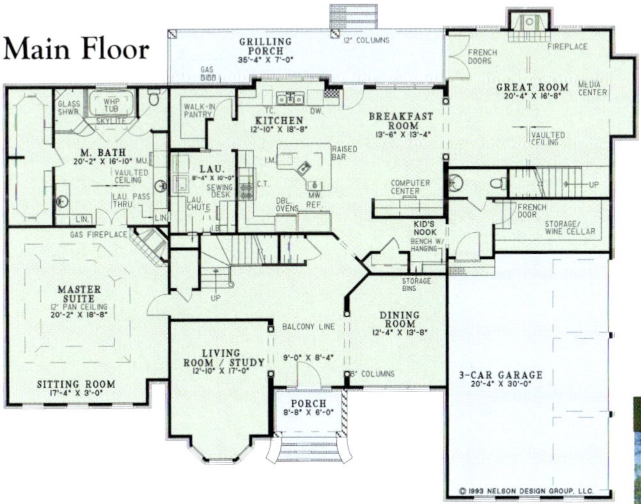

584 Hickory Place

Width: 79' 10"
Depth: 60' 6"
Main Floor: 2,861 sq. ft.
Upper Floor: 1,600 sq. ft.
Total Living: 4,461 sq. ft.*
*Bonus: 250 sq. ft.
Main Ceiling: 10 ft.
Upper Ceiling: 9 ft.

Bedrooms: 5
Baths: 4 1/2
Foundation: Crawl, Slab, Optional Basement, Optional Daylight Basement
Plan Options: page 93

Price Tier: G

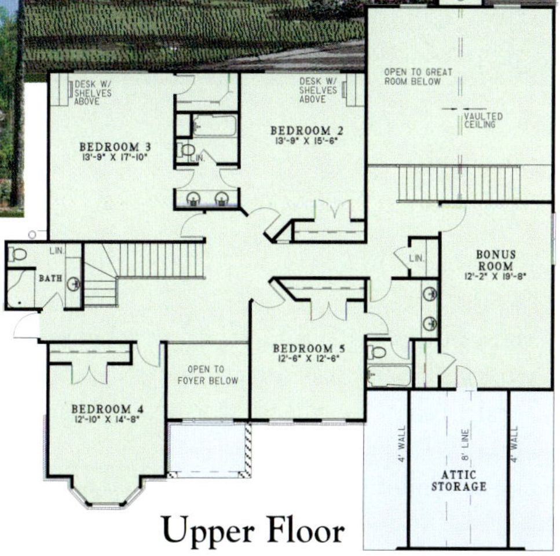

Upper Floor

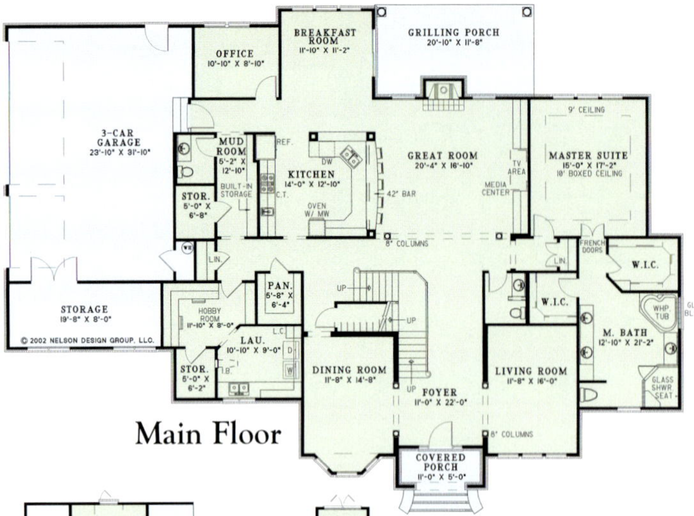

Main Floor

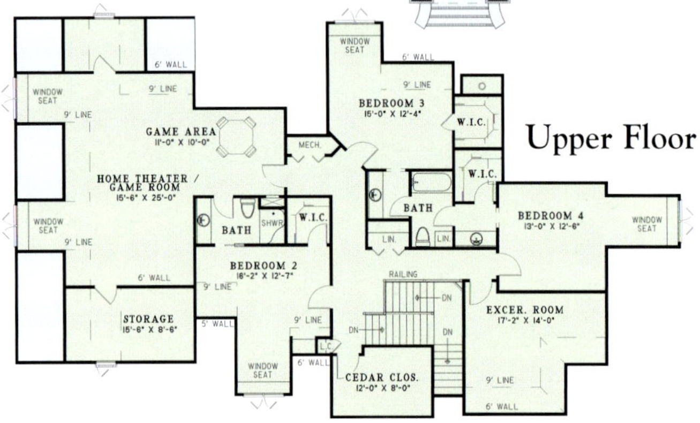

Upper Floor

647 Dogwood Avenue

Width: 87' 8"
Depth: 60' 4"
Main Floor: 2,954 sq. ft.
Upper Floor: 1,534 sq. ft.
Total Living: 4,488 sq. ft.*
*Bonus: 601 sq. ft.
Main Ceiling: 10 ft.
Upper Ceiling: 9 ft.

Bedrooms: 4
Baths: 3 full, 2 half
Foundation: Crawl, Slab, Optional Basement, Optional Daylight Basement
Plan Options: page 93

Price Tier: G

To order call toll free 1-800-590-2423

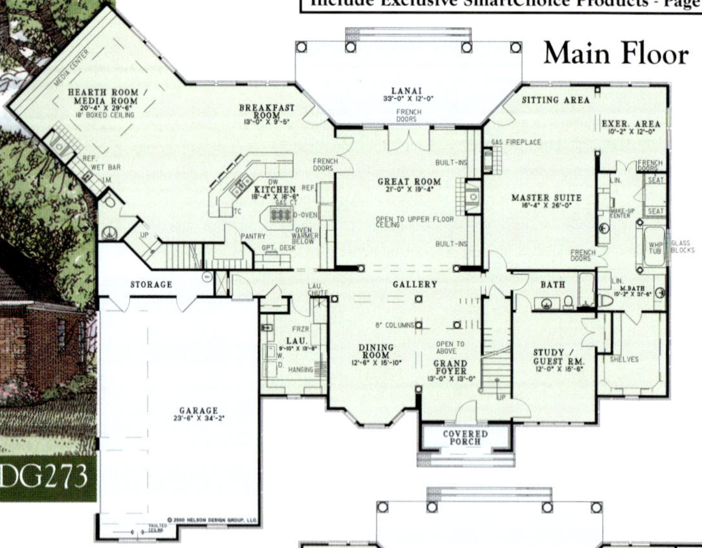

Main Floor

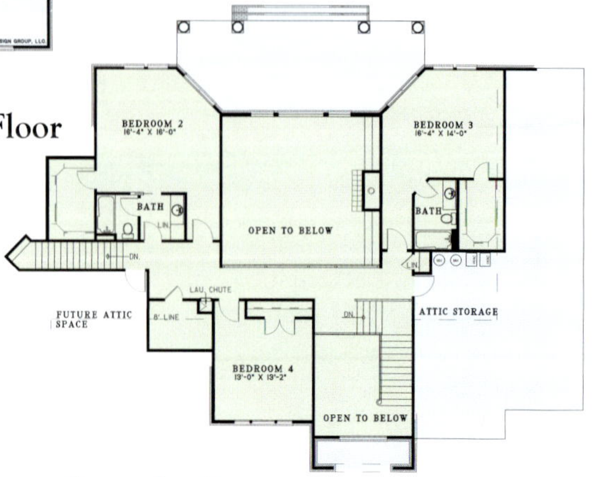

Upper Floor

273 Dogwood Avenue

Width: 96' 10"
Depth: 76' 6"
Main Floor: 3,526 sq. ft.
Upper Floor: 1,347 sq. ft.
Total Living: 4,873 sq. ft.
Main Ceiling: 9 ft.
Upper Ceiling: 8 ft.

Bedrooms: 4
Baths: 4 1/2
Foundation: Crawl, Slab, Basement, Daylight Basement
Plan Options: page 93

Price Tier: G

Similar plans can be viewed and ordered at www.nelsondesigngroup.com

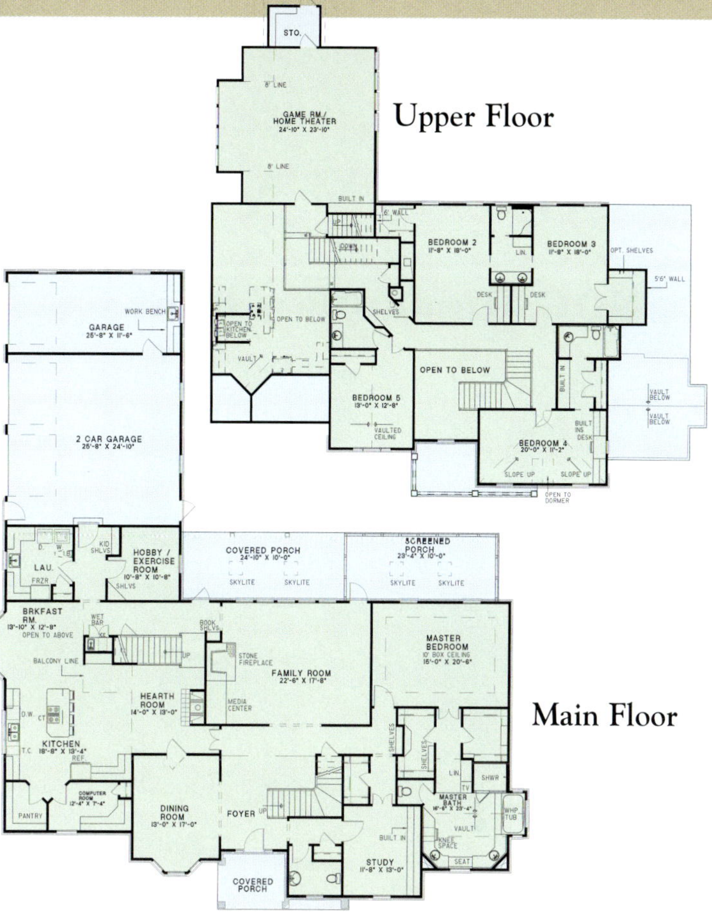

138 Cherry Street

Width: 81' 6"
Depth: 93' 2"
Main Floor: 3,276 sq. ft.
Upper Floor: 2,272 sq. ft.
Total Living: 5,548 sq. ft.
Main Ceiling: 9 ft.
Upper Ceiling: 9 ft.

Bedrooms: 5
Baths: 4 1/2
Foundation: Crawl, Slab, Optional Basement, Optional Daylight Basement
Plan Options: page 93

Price Tier: G

Any plan can be modified to your specific needs - Call 1-800-590-2423 for pricing

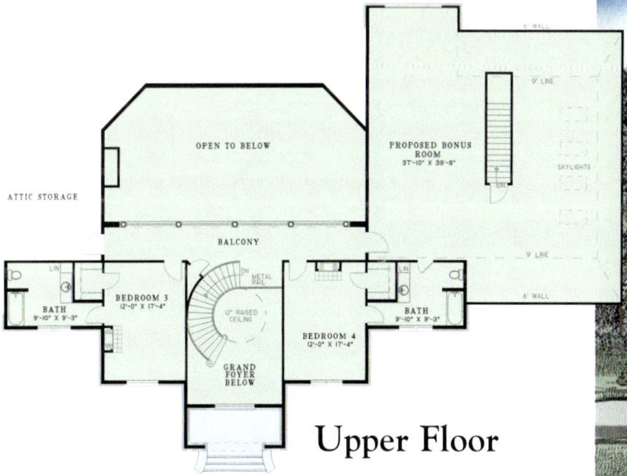

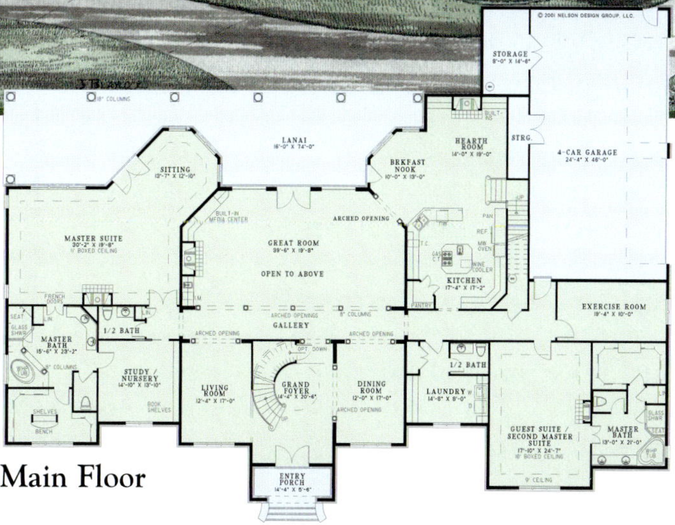

621 Birchwood Lane

Width: 117' 8"
Depth: 84' 8"
Main Floor: 5,338 sq. ft.
Upper Floor: 1,050 sq. ft.
Total Living: 6,388 sq. ft.*
*Bonus: 1,460 sq. ft.
Main Ceiling: 10 ft.
Upper Ceiling: 9 ft.

Bedrooms: 4
Baths: 4 full, 2 half
Foundation: Crawl, Slab, Optional Basement, Optional Daylight Basement
Plan Options: page 93

Price Tier: G

NDG MARKETING PRODUCTS

w w w . n e l s o n d e s i g n g r o u p . c o m

NDG Home Plan Books

Nelson Design Group wants to ensure that our customers, whether consumers or builders, have the most helpful designs available. At NDG, we are constantly developing new plan publications in addition to our permanent collection. These books are valuable tools in selecting the home of your dreams, providing easy-to-read floor plans and specs, and detailed artistic renderings in full color. Each book showcases new plan collections, with minimal duplication, for optimum variety.

Builder Edition - Volume I
(Black/White – 80 pages) **$10**

Builder Edition - Volume II
(Black/White – 80 pages) **$10**

"New Beginnings"
(Full Color – 156 pages) **$15**

Builder's Special Edition I
(Full Color – 288 pages) **$20**

Builder's Special Edition II
(Full Color – 288 pages) **$20**

Builder's Special Edition III
(Full Color – 304 pages) **$20**

All 6 Plan Books **$50**
(shipping and handling not included)

Big Image On A Small Budget!

View each of these products at
www.nelsondesigngroup.com

Feature Sheets **$50**
100 sheets/pack - 8.5" x 11" customized color rendering with floor plan, your color logo and customized bullet points. 20% discount with 2 packs or more of same plan.

Framed Prints
Professionally framed and matted 20" x 24" color renderings customized with your logo, floor plan and bullet point features.

Black Metal Frame **$89**
Wooden Frame **$89**
Gold Frame **$150**

Complete Yard Sign Kit **$299**
24" x 36", poster in vertical format, laminated, weatherproofed, and customized to display in front of your construction site.

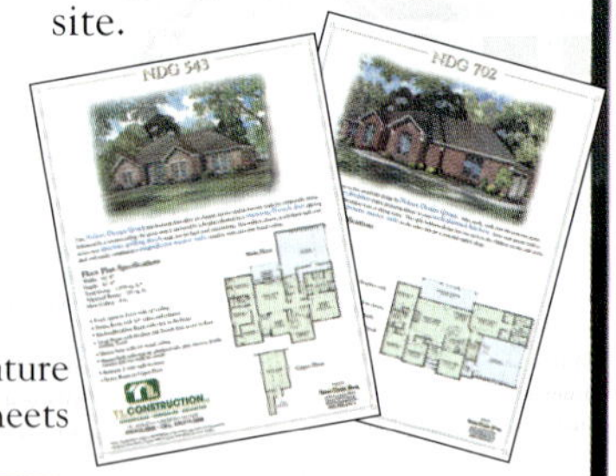

Feature Sheets

Complete Yard Sign Kit

Framed & Matted Prints

Interior & Outdoor Signage
Brochures
Logo and Artwork
Back-Lit Signage
Specialty Printing
Video Presentations
3-D Virtual & Interactive Tours

Promotion,
Ad Placement,
Public Relations
And More!

NDG HOME PLAN OPTIONS

www.nelsondesigngroup.com

Not only do we have numerous designs created for various sized homes, we encourage the modification of our stock plans to meet personal specifications. Nelson Design Group will help you fulfill your dreams with a customized computer area, media center, hearth room, privacy nooks or whatever your needs entail.

Architectural in-house sealed prints are available for an additional fee with the exception of CA. Please contact our customer service for further information. 1-800-590-2423

MODIFICATION PACKAGES

include a setup and consultation fee, the cost of the reproducible (vellums) and the estimated hourly design fees. All quotes are based on original stock plan price tiers and created on a per plan basis according to criteria provided by the customer. To receive an estimated modification quote and completion time please submit your changes in writing. Modification requests can be faxed to **(870)931-5792** or emailed to **info@nelsondesigngroup.com.**

Upon receiving a modification request, NDG will send a modification agreement including fees, payment options and completion schedule.

Code Compliance: Our plans are drawn to meet the International Residential Code. Many states and counties amend the codes to adapt to their area. Consult your local building officials to determine the plan, code and site requirements for your area.

FOUNDATION ALTERATIONS

Optional Basement Foundation - $250.00
Optional Daylight Basement Foundation - $250.00
Monolithic Slab - $250.00
I-Joists - $250.00
I-Joists with Optional Basement - $350.00

WALL OPTIONS

2 x 4 to 2 x 6 Complete Wall Conversion - $250.00
2 x 4 to Concrete Block (up to 2,499 sq. ft.) - $450.00
(2,500 sq. ft. and up) - $650.00

All NDG plans are available for Logix ICF conversion. (Excluding Log Homes) Call for Pricing.

EXTERIOR ALTERATIONS

Siding to Brick - $250.00
Brick to Siding - $250.00

GARAGE ALTERATIONS

Side Load to Front Entry - $250.00
Front Entry to Side Load - $250.00
Two Car to Three Car - $375.00
Three Car to Two Car - $375.00

CEILING ALTERATIONS

8 ft. to 9 ft. - $250.00
9 ft. to 8 ft. - $250.00

ROOF ALTERATIONS

Hip to Gable - $500.00
Gable to Hip - $500.00

For Architectural Stamps and additional modifications not listed, please call **1-800-590-2423.**

Please note prices are subject to change.

Nelson Design Group LLC

RESIDENTIAL PLANNERS - DESIGNERS

NDG HOME PLAN CONTENTS

w w w . n e l s o n d e s i g n g r o u p . c o m

FOUNDATION PLAN

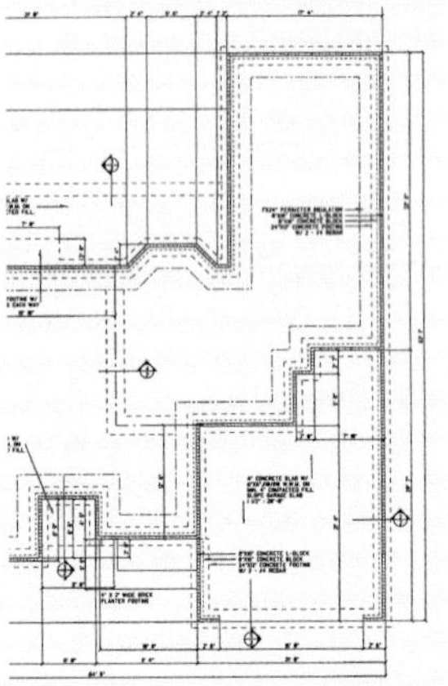

(1/4" or 1/2" = 1')
Most plans are available with a slab or crawl space foundation. Optional walkout style basement (three walls masonry with a wood framed side or rear wall) or full basement available if plan allows, at an additional cost. Please call for details.
*When a basement or walkout basement is chosen, square footage will be altered, increasing the depth or width of home, where applicable.

FLOOR PLAN(S)

(1/4" = 1')
Each home plan includes the floor plan showing the dimensioned locations of walls, doors and windows.

ELEVATIONS

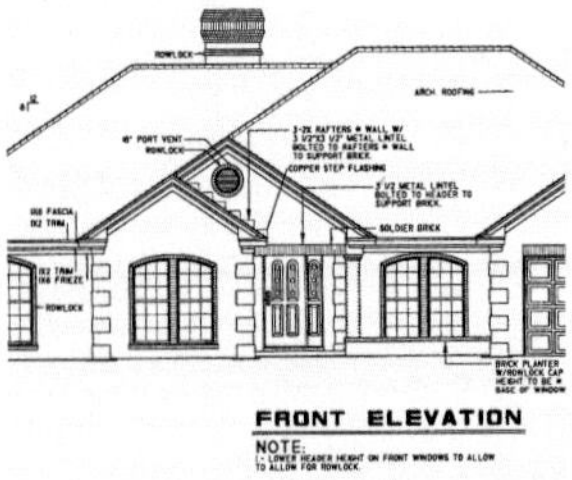

(1/4" = 1')
All plans include the exterior elevations (front, rear, right and left) that show and describe the finished material of the house.

DETAIL SECTION(S)

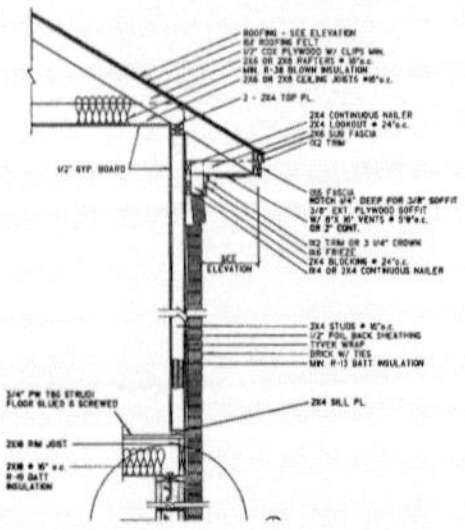

(1/4" or 1/2" = 1')
The exterior wall sections are vertical cuts through the outside wall showing how the foundation, stud wall, ceiling joists and roof rafters are all constructed. Materials used are specified.

KITCHEN & BATH CABINET ELEVATIONS

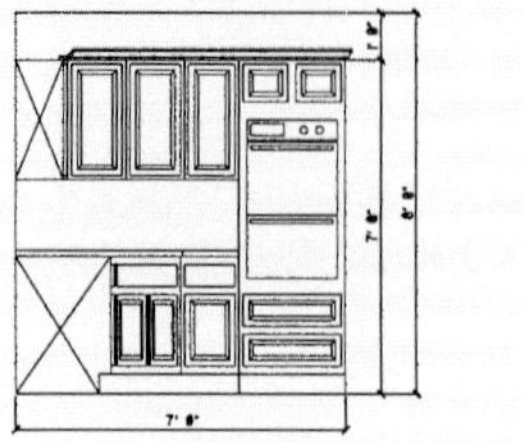

(1/2" = 1')
Kitchen and bath cabinet elevations show the arrangement and size of each cabinet and other fixtures in the room. These drawings give basic information that can be used to create customized layouts with a cabinet manufacturer.

ROOF OVERVIEW PLAN

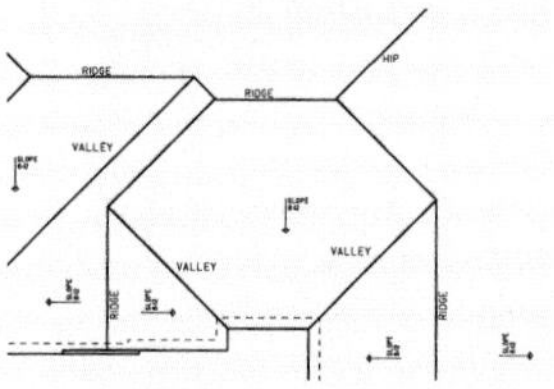

(1/4" = 1')
This is a "bird's eye" view showing the roof slopes, ridges, valleys and any saddles.

MISCELLANEOUS DETAILS

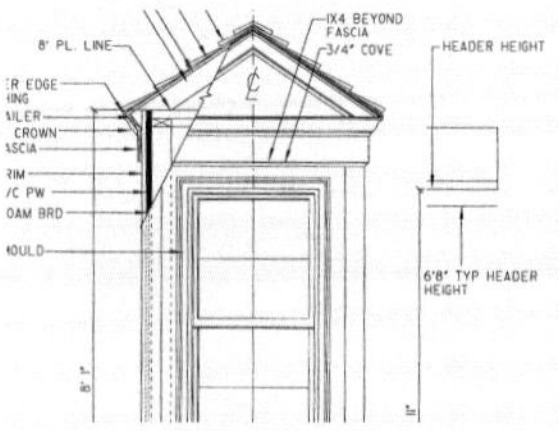

(3/4" = 1')
These are included for many interior and exterior conditions that require more specific information for their construction.

ELECTRICAL PLANS

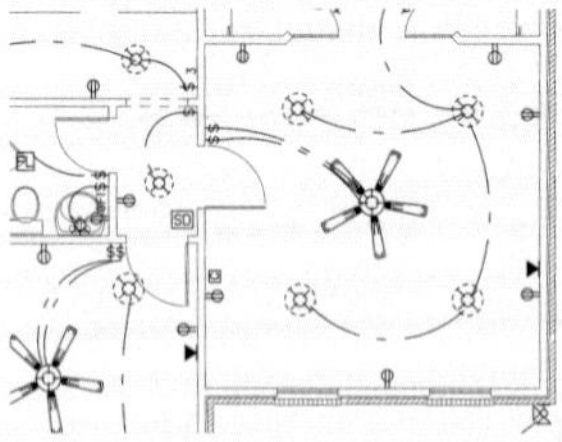

The electrical plans shown are suggested layouts of lighting and outlet placements, along with other appliances that the designer chooses to best fit the plan.

Nelson Design Group, LLC Home Plans can carry an architect stamp for an additional fee. CA is an exception.

Code Compliance: Our plans are drawn to meet the International Residential Code. Many states and counties amend the codes to adapt to their area. Consult your local building officials to determine the plan, code and site requirements for your area.

Heated and Cooled Square Footage calculations are made from outside the exterior frame wall and do not include decks, porches, garages, basements, attics, fireplaces, etc. We include two story and vaulted areas only once in the calculations of the first floor. Stairs are counted once. Balconies and open walkways in two-story and vaulted areas are included in square footage of the second floor.

For Technical Assistance Call 1-800-590-2423

NDG HOME PLAN SERVICES

w w w . n e l s o n d e s i g n g r o u p . c o m

FLOOR FRAMING PLANS

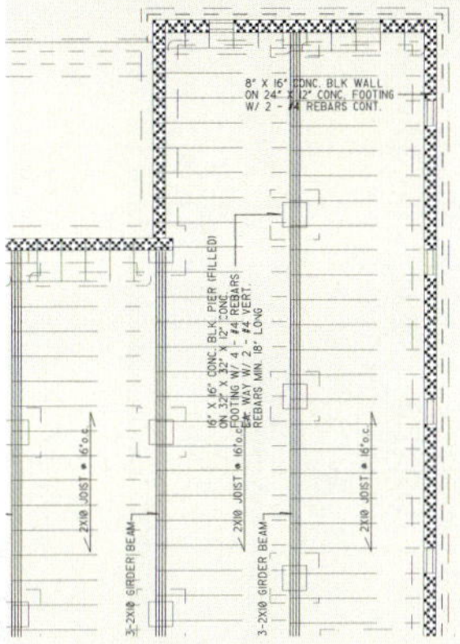

(1/4" = 1'-0")
Each floor framing plan on crawlspace foundation only shows each floor joist indicating the layout and spacing. All beams are labeled and sized.

$100.00

Basements & upper floors are open web trusses. Layouts are provided by truss manufacturer

CROSS SECTION

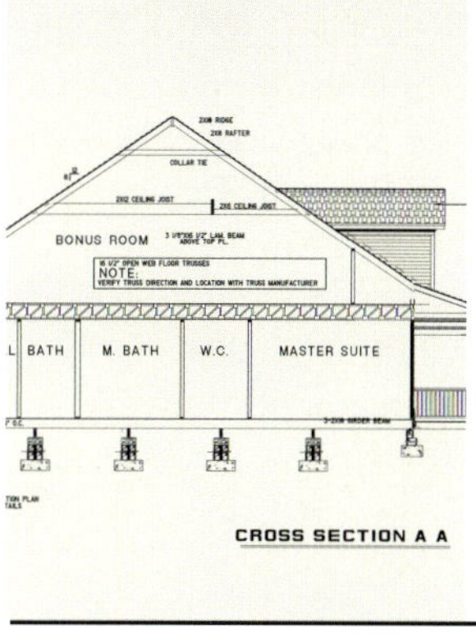

Complete cut through pertinent areas of the house with the location of beams floor joists and other relevant elements for ease of understanding of the complete construction of the home.

$100.00

CEILING JOIST FRAMING PLAN

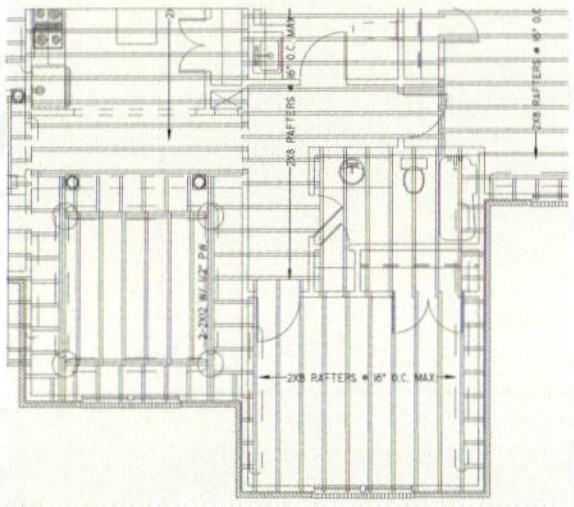

(1/4" = 1'-0")
The ceiling joist framing plan shows each ceiling joist indicating the size and spacing. All beams are labeled and sized.

$100.00

RIGHT-READABLE REVERSED PLANS

Right-readable reversed plans are available should you wish to build your home reverse of the one shown in our book or on our website. The lettering and dimensions appear right reading. From the total number of sets ordered, all plans will be reversed. Check the appropriate area on the order form or let us know when placing your order.

ROOF FRAMING PLAN

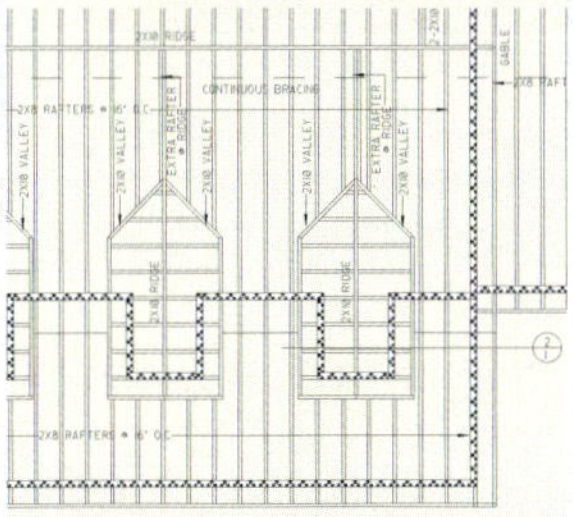

(1/4" = 1'-0")
The roof framing plan shows each rafter, valley, hip and ridge indicating the size, spacing and length. All beams are labeled and sized.

$100.00

REPRODUCIBLES

With the purchase of a reproducible set (vellums), a license and copyright release are also provided. Similarly, the purchase of reproducible home plans carries the same copyright protection as mentioned in this book. It is generally allowed to make up to a maximum of 10 copies for the construction of a single dwelling only. To use any plans more than once, and to avoid any copyright licenses infringement, it is necessary to contact Nelson Design Group, LLC to receive a release and a license for any extended usage. Nelson Design Group, LLC will make special provisions for plan usage within developments when previous arrangements have been made directly with Nelson Design Group, LLC.

MISCELLANEOUS FRAMING DETAILS

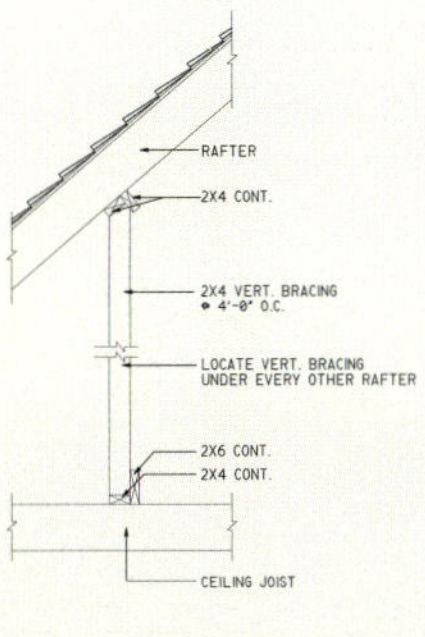

Each framing plan sheet includes any framing details that are needed (boxed ceiling details, connection details, etc.) All of the framing is designed using conventional framing materials. Open web trusses are used in most one-and-a-half story and two-story plans.

CAD DISKS

CAD Disks are available on all NDG plans, with the exception of our Jim Barna Log System Collection. Standard formats are DWG and DXF. See order form for pricing.

Nelson Design Group LLC
RESIDENTIAL PLANNERS - DESIGNERS

NDG HOME PLAN SERVICES

www.nelsondesigngroup.com

TRU-COST ESTIMATES & SOFTWARE

Nelson Design Group has developed the Tru-Cost Estimating system of estimates and software as a valuable tool for builders to use in the planning and construction of new homes. We have combined a thorough database of items required for construction. We offer three different options for our customers by providing estimates for all of our Stock Plans, as well as Modified and Custom Plans. Our Custom Estimate is not only available for our plans, it's also offered for our customer's plans. The Custom Estimate service allows the customer to modify or change any of the pricing or materials they may wish to use.

Tru-Cost Estimates	
NDG Stock Plan Estimate	$125.00
Revised Estimate for NDG Stock Plan	$250.00
Custom Estimate starting at	$500.00
Tru-Cost Estimating Software	**$299.00**

Tru-Cost Estimates for Logix ICF Conversion
Call 1-800-590-2423 for Pricing

COPYRIGHT LAW

Reproduction of the illustration and working drawings of these home plans, either in whole or in part, including any form and/or preparation of derivative works thereof, for any reason without prior written permission is strictly prohibited. The purchase of a set of home plans in no way transfers any copyright or other ownership interest in it to the buyer except for a limited license to use that set of home plans for the construction of one, and only one, dwelling unit. The purchase of an additional set (s) of that home plan at a reduced price from the original set or as part of a multiple set package does not convey to the buyer a license to construct more than one dwelling. This is also the case with reproducible vellum, CAD disks or any multimedia.

Similarly, the purchase of reproducible vellum carries the same copyright protection as mentioned above. It is generally allowed to make up to a maximum of 10 copies for the construction of a single dwelling only. To use any plans more than once, and to avoid any copyright licenses infringement, it is necessary to contact the plan designer to receive a release and a license for any extended usage. Nelson Design Group, LLC will make special provisions for plan usage within developments when previous arrangements have been made directly with Nelson Design Group, LLC.

Whereas a purchaser of reproducibles is granted license to make copies, it should be noted that as copyright material, making photocopies from blueprints is illegal.

Copyright and licensing of home plans for construction exist to protect all parties. It respects and supports the intellectual property of the original architect or designer. Copyright law has been reinforced over the past few years. Willful infringement could cause settlements for statutory damages up to $150,000.00 plus attorney fees, damages and loss of profits.

NDG ORDER INFORMATION

www.nelsondesigngroup.com

BLUEPRINT PRICING

Price Tier	Square Feet	One Set	Four Sets	Eight Sets	Twelve Sets	Repro Sets	CAD Disk
A	0-1499	$500	$550	$575	$625	$685	$1,160
B	1500-1999	$530	$575	$625	$675	$730	$1,250
C	2000-2499	$575	$625	$675	$725	$800	$1,350
D	2500-2999	$650	$700	$750	$825	$925	$1,450
E	3000-3499	$750	$800	$825	$900	$1,000	$1,625
F	3500-3999	$800	$825	$875	$925	$1,025	$1,675
G	4000 and up	$900	$950	$1,000	$1,050	$1,125	$1,725

*Prices are subject to change. Special or grouped plans may vary in price. *No CAD for Log Home Plans.*

ONE SET (stamped "not for construction")
Recommended for preview study

FOUR SETS
Recommended for bidding

EIGHT SETS
Recommended for construction

TWELVE SETS
Recommended for multiple bids

REPRODUCIBLE SETS
Recommended for construction/modifications

CAD Disks*
DXF/DWG Files

Additional Sets - Additional individual sets of plan ordered at point of sale are **$40** each.

Right Readable-Reversed Plans - A **$50** surcharge. From the total number of sets you order above, all plans will be reversed. You pay only **$50**. Note: All plans are produced using computers, and all text is reversed as well.

SHIPPING AND HANDLING

Number Of Sets	1-3	4-7	8 or more	Repro	CAD Disk
U.S. Regular (5-6 business days)	$20.00	$25.00	$30.00	$20.00	$17.50
U.S. Express (2-3 business days)	$40.00	$45.00	$50.00	$40.00	$35.00
Canada Regular (5-7 business days)	$45.00	$50.00	$55.00	$45.00	$40.00
Canada Express (2-4 business days)	$60.00	$65.00	$70.00	$60.00	$55.00
Overseas/Airmail (7-10 business days)	$80.00	$90.00	$100.00	$80.00	$70.00

All Nelson Design Group, LLC sales are non-credit purchases. The total amount is due when your order is placed. Orders may not be returned or exchanged. All orders are final.

CUSTOMER INFORMATION

Name: ______________________

Company Name: ______________________

Address: ______________________

City: ______________ State: ________ Zip: ________

Phone: ______________ Fax: ______________

E-mail Address: ______________________

Credit Card #: ______________ Exp. Date: ________

☐ VISA ☐ MasterCard ☐ AmEx ☐ Discover

☐ Check/Money Order Enclosed (U.S. Funds)

Source Code: **NDG1Rel-05**	Plan #	Plan #	Plan #
Price Tier			
Number of Sets/CAD/Reproducible Sets			
Blueprint Cost			
Additional Sets @ $40 each			
Right Readable-Reversed Sets @ $50			
Tru-Cost Estimating @ $125			
☐ Crawl			
☐ Slab			
☐ Basement			
☐ Basement (Opt.) @ $250.00			
☐ Daylight Basement			
☐ Daylight Basement (Opt.) @ $250.00			
Tru-Cost Software @ $299.00			
☐ Other			
Sub-Total			
Shipping & Handling			
TOTAL			

MAIL ORDER TO:

Nelson Design Group LLC

RESIDENTIAL PLANNERS - DESIGNERS

2200 Fowler Ave. • Suite D
Jonesboro, AR 72401

Phone: 870-931-5777
Fax: 870-931-5792

ORDER ONLINE:

www.nelsondesigngroup.com

FOR ORDERING & TECHNICAL ASSISTANCE CALL:

800-590-2423

Landscaping...

the Finishing Touch for Your New Home

NDG Stock Landscape PLANS

Specially Designed for your new home...

Just imagine!

NDG Stock Landscape Plans are designed by a professional landscape architect for your specific home. Take your plans to any landscape service and they'll do the rest. Or, if you have a green thumb, our plans make it easy to do it yourself.

Here's what you get:

- Professionally designed plans by a licensed landscape architect
- Two 18" x 24" copies of your planting plan
- Full color Planting Booklet with photos, planting specifications, sizes and quantities

Only $300.00

BHMdesign

Nelson Design Group LLC

RESIDENTIAL PLANNERS - DESIGNERS

Call Now!

800-590-2423

www.nelsondesigngroup.com

NDG HOME PLAN INDEX

www.nelsondesigngroup.com

NDG Commercial Division INC.

ARCHITECTURE & PLANNING

ARE YOUR DESIGN DEMANDS CHANGING?

Let NDG Commercial Division, Inc., meet your immediate goals, as well as, the requirements and ongoing needs of an ever changing market.

We are defining new ideas everyday.

Office - NDG-C109

Our Stock Plans and Traditional Services provide a shorter design schedule, creative solutions and reduced design fees.

We have the imagination and creative skills to understand and execute the complex process of design.

PROJECT TYPES - **Commercial, Shopping Centers, Multi-Family, Religious, Lodging...**

Office - NDG-C137

SERVICES

Conceptual Designs
Master Planning
Space Planning
Permit Coordination
Code Research
Construction Documents
Interiors

NDG Commercial Division will -

- ***Save you time***
- ***Make key project decisions***
- ***Work with your Consultants***
- ***Focus on your Business needs***
- ***See the "Big Picture"***

Matt Silas, AIA

Principal Architect and President of **NDG Commercial Division, Inc.**, has the necessary experience and background having produced a variety of design types for commercial structures.

NDG Commercial Division, Inc., works closely with other members of the construction industry in design that provides the client with an exceptional product.

www.ndgcommercialdivision.com

Call **1-866-932-5910** For Architectural Services

Let **NDG Commercial Division, Inc.,** create a design for the total development

Comfortable, Cost Effective, Creative

Finally a marketing firm that caters to BUILDERS needs.

Full Color Interior Signs
Yard Sign Kits
Full Color Feature Sheets
3-D Virtual Reality Tours
Full Color Brochures
Full Color Development Brochures
Web Site Design
Multi-Media Support
Full Color Collection Portfolios
Grand Openings
Home Development Consultation
Model Home Marketing Materials
Watercolor Architectural Renderings
Ad Design & Placement
News Release & Placement
Builder Identity Packages
Home Plan Book Production
Public Relations & More!
Logo Creation & Graphic Design
Full Color Interior Signs
Yard Sign Kits
Full Color Feature Sheets
3-D Virtual Reality Tours
Full Color Brochures
Full Color Development Brochures
Web Site Design
Multi-Media Support
Full Color Collection Portfolios
Grand Openings
Home Development Consultation

The Bottom Line...

We can provide you with everything you need to sell your homes.

BUILDERS Marketing Firm LLC

Building Your Image Through Advertising

These products & many more!

Builders Marketing Firm, LLC can readily and **affordably** help your **business grow**. From logo creation to complete identity packages, we have **experience** in providing professional materials that will help in promoting your company. In todays competitive market **first impressions** are of the utmost importance and **presentation is everything**. Our affordable professionally developed promotional tools are **designed to work for you**, to promote your projects before, during, and after construction.

Website

Feature Sheets

Letterhead

Envelopes

Bus. Cards

Watercolor Renderings

Development Signage

Brochures

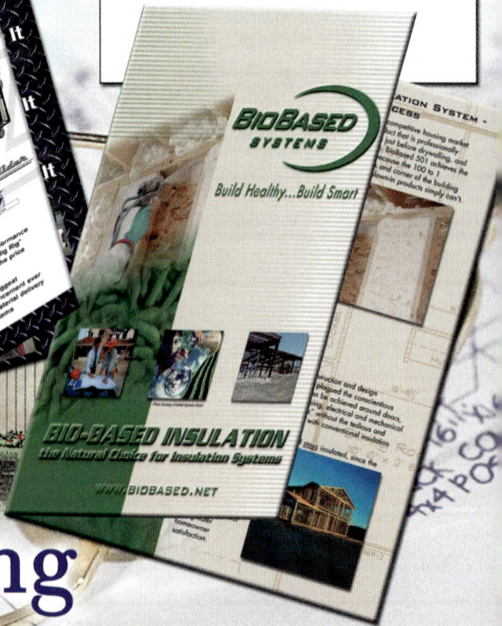

Printing Services

Real world Marketing that Works

Call toll free today for your Free Information Kit 1.866.934.7877

Model Home Marketing Materials

NDG CORPORATE PARTNERS

www.nelsondesigngroup.com

As a leading national home design firm, we want to make sure our customers have a "support-system" and resources to help them make educated choices during the critical planning stages. Our Exclusive NDG Corporate Partners will assist you in making these "smart choices" for your new home whether you're building a starter home, multi-family investment or your dream home. The new construction phase is the right time to incorporate family-friendly amenities, structured wiring, built-in media and products that will add to your quality of life....adding value to your new home. You must consider incorporating energy efficient products that will ultimately save money on monthly utility bills while increasing the value of your investment. We highly recommend our **NDG Corporate Partner SmartChoice Products** because we know these products are right for your home and we've conveniently specified them into our design...your new home.

Company Name	Product	Page
84 Lumber	Lumber Company	127
Amarr Garage Doors	Garage Doors	115
Beam	Central Vacuum Systems	121
BioBased Insulation	Natural Soy-based Blown Insulation	125
ClosetMaid	Closet Storage Systems	112
DoorSaver	All New Doorstop	116
Gladiator GarageWorks	Garage Storage & Organizing Systems	104
Jason Hydrotherapy	Bathing Systems	113
JBL	Home Theater & Multi-Room Audio	107
Jeld-Wen	Windows & Doors	118, 119
KitchenAid	Home Appliances	129
LG Hi-Macs	Acrylic Solid Surface & Sinks	110
L.J. Smith Stair Systems	Stair Systems	120
Lennox	Comfort Systems	123
Logix	Insulated Concrete Forms	105
M-Boss	Pressed Metal Ceiling Tile Panels	122
Merillat	Cabinetry	128
Hanson Brick	Brick	126
Pioneer	Home Theater, Plasma TV's, Electronics	108, 109
Pittsburgh Corning	Glass Block Systems	114
Rev-A-Shelf	Kitchen & Bath Cabinet Accessories	124
TrimJoist	Floor Trusses - Open-web/IBeams	111
Vantage Controls	Automation/Lighting Control	106
Weslock	Levers/Locksets, Door Handles	117

Gladiator™ GarageWorks by Whirlpool Corporation.

In a word, Impressive.

"Our finished garage is as impressive as our home."

GLADIATOR™
GARAGEWORKS
by Whirlpool Corporation

A finished garage may be a top priority for your new home. For automotive, sports and gardening enthusiasts, Gladiator™ GarageWorks by Whirlpool Corporation transforms the garage with dependable appliances, as well as rugged and sleek tread plate faced flooring and modular components.

Enjoy a beautifully finished garage with Gladiator™ GarageWorks.

Learn more at 866-342-4089 or www.GladiatorGW.com.

Why our competition is seeing red.

Thermal image of a conventionally built home showing heat loss across the entire wall.

Thermal image of a LOGIX™ home shows minimal heat loss, resulting in lower energy bills.

Unlike traditional walls, LOGIX™ ICF can **prevent costly heat loss** and significantly **lower your energy bills.**

Introducing LOGIX™ ICF, a wall system with the unbeatable strength of concrete and insulating properties of foam. LOGIX™ uses 2 3/4" thick foam exclusively in all form sizes. Other ICF brands use a variety of foam thicknesses from 1 1/2" to 2 1/2". LOGIX™ ICF gives you an outstanding wall system that's long-lasting, quick to build, sound-proofed, energy-efficient and has a 3-hour fire resistance rating.

Don't settle for less. For more information about LOGIX™ ICF call 1-888-706-7709 today.
All NDG home plans can be coverted to the LOGIX™ System. (Excluding log homes)

logixicf.com

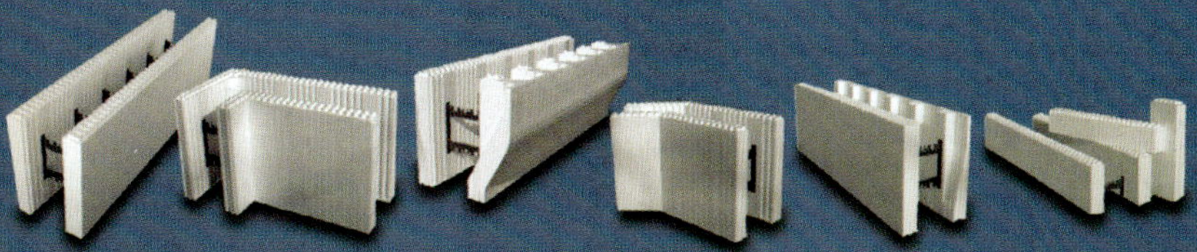

LOGIX INSULATED CONCRETE FORMS
Good. Solid. Logix.™

COMPLETE HOME AUTOMATION AND LIGHTING CONTROL

1061 SOUTH 800 EAST
OREM, UTAH 84097

800.555.9891
801.224.0355 FAX

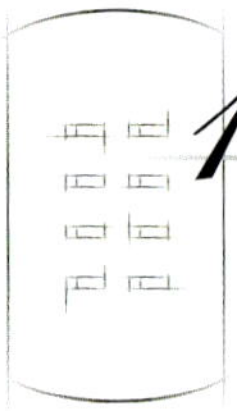

1 WHAT IS AUTOMATION?

Automation by Vantage integrates complex home devices into one simple and intelligent system. Lights and blinds automatically adjust based on outside lighting conditions. A bedside button ensures that the garage door is closed and that all lights gradually change to your preset, night time levels. A single movie button fades your lights and activates your audio/video equipment, just like the movie theater. A midnight trip to the bathroom activates a soft night light. Vantage automation is convenience, simplicity, and comfort.

2 WHAT CAN IT DO FOR ME?

Vantage automation and lighting control systems simplify your life. They reduce energy costs and provide peace of mind. Multiple and complex remote controls are eliminated. Vantage automates your heating and cooling systems without the need to manually adjust from one season to another. Securely access any of your home systems via the Internet. Ensure that lights behave as if someone is home while you are on vacation. View visitors at the front door from the convenience of your kitchen. Flash every light in your house if you encounter an intruder. Vantage improves your quality of life.

3 HOW DO I GET IT?

Vantage automation systems are available from qualified electrical, audio/video, and automation dealers throughout the world. Cost effective Vantage automation packages typically begin at about three dollars a square foot. This is often less money, but a greater value than other home investments such as floor coverings, appliances, or home electronics. Contact a Vantage dealer today for a system that will meet your needs and fit your budget.

VANTAGE
Your First Choice in Automation & Lighting Control

contact a dealer at
www.vantagecontrols.com

PRO SOUND COMES HOME TO RESIDENTIAL NEW CONSTRUCTION AND RETROFITS.

SPECIFYING AND INSTALLING JBL FOR RESIDENTIAL SOUND SYSTEMS NOT ONLY GIVES YOU THE BENEFITS OF OUR RENOWNED AUDIO, AND REPUTATION FOR RELIABILITY. IT PUTS YOU IN THE COMPANY OF LEADING PROFESSIONALS IN THE MUSIC AND MOVIE INDUSTRIES WHO CONSISTENTLY CHOOSE JBL FOR WORLD-CLASS INSTALLATIONS.

IN 1928, WHEN JAMES B. LANSING HELPED MAKE MOVIES TALK, QUALITY SOUND REPRODUCTION WAS LITERALLY UNHEARD OF. THE COMPANY LANSING FOUNDED WENT ON TO HELP DEFINE THE CONCEPT OF HIGH FIDELITY. WE HAVEN'T LOOKED BACK SINCE.

TODAY, JBL IS THE SYSTEM OF CHOICE FOR MORE THAN 80% OF ALL DOLBY® DIGITAL CINEMA INSTALLATIONS. WE'RE IN THE FINEST CONCERT HALLS AND AT MAJOR ROCK CONCERTS, AND WE CONTINUE TO PRODUCE THE MONITOR SPEAKER OF CHOICE FOR TOP RECORDING STUDIOS. JBL'S RESIDENTIAL PRODUCTS ARE FURTHER EXAMPLES OF OUR CONTINUED COMMITMENT TO ADVANCED SOUND REPRODUCTION TECHNOLOGY.

NOTHING QUITE COMPARES TO LISTENING TO YOUR FAVORITE MUSIC OR WATCHING THE LATEST MOVIES WHILE EXPERIENCING ALL THE INTENSITY AND NUANCES OF A LIVE PERFORMANCE... RIGHT AT HOME!

WE'RE NOT JUST BRINGING PRO SOUND HOME – WE'RE HELPING YOU TO PLACE IT RIGHT INTO WALLS, CEILINGS AND PATIOS.

IN-WALL AND CEILING LOUDSPEAKERS | BOOKSHELF LOUDSPEAKERS | FLOORSTANDING LOUDSPEAKERS | POWERED SUBWOOFERS | SURROUND CINEMA LOUDSPEAKER SYSTEMS | STUDIO MONITORS | ALL-WEATHER LOUDSPEAKERS

For more information, call 818.830.8757 or visit www.jbl.com.

JBL®

PRO SOUND COMES HOME™

JBL Consumer Products
250 Crossways Park Drive, Woodbury, NY 11797
8500 Balboa Boulevard, Northridge, CA 91329
818.830.8757 www.jbl.com

H A Harman International Company

Pioneer sound.vision.soul

BUILD YOUR DREAM HOME AND THE HOME THEATER OF YOUR DREAMS... TOGETHER

Are you aware that many lenders will allow you to include your home theater system in with your financing? Now you can enjoy a spectacular home theater experience the moment you walk through the door. By installing your Pioneer® recommended home theater while your dream house is being built, our authorized Pioneer installation professional will flawlessly integrate your system in with your living space. This way you'll benefit from a custom solution, seamlessly crafted to satisfy your exact requirements.

For more information, call

1-800-590-2423

© 2002 Pioneer Electronics (USA) Inc, Long Beach, CA
Pioneer
Pioneer products feature the most advanced technology to deliver the ultimate home theater experience.
• True High Definition Large Screen Displays
- 43" and 50" Plasma Monitors Only 4" Deep
- High Definition Ready Projection TVs From 53" to 64"
• High Performance Multi-Channel Audio and Video Components
- AV Surround Sound Receivers and Amplifiers for Every Size Room and Every Application
- Award-Winning DVD Recording and Playback Components, PureCinema Progressive Scan, DVD Audio and Super Audio CD Capability
Blossfeldt

The new standard is solid surface countertops, thanks to LG HI-MACS.

15 Year Fully Transferable WARRANTY

The new Volcanics Collection from LG HI-MACS adds eight colors to its already expansive palette, offering a unique beauty to kitchens across America. LG HI-MACS has combined the durability and performance of acrylic solid surface with an unsurpassed elegance. Backed by the only 15 year fully transferable warranty in the industry, you will receive a superior product with greater value.

The Volcanics Collection from LG HI-MACS. Engineered to be the new standard in America's homes.

LG | 1.866.LGHI.MACS | www.lgvolcanics.com | LG HI-MACS Volcanics

JASON®
HYDROTHERAPY
Hydrotherapy Bathing of Your Choice:
WHIRLPOOL • AIRMASSEUR™ • AIR-WHIRLPOOL
JASON INTERNATIONAL, INC.
8328 MacArthur Drive
North Little Rock, AR 72118
800.255.5766
jasoninternational.com

There's nothing that accents a room quite like real glass block from Pittsburgh Corning. Glass block adds beauty, light and class to any home, whether it's used in a wall, window or shower. Plus, our durable, scratch-resistant, 100% real glass block comes in a variety of patterns and shapes. Select from our pre-designed Shower Systems, pre-assembled LightWise® Windows, or draw on the expertise of our network of distributors/installers to take your ideas from concept to completion. For more information on creating a unique statement with glass block or to locate a distributor/dealer near you, visit www.pcglassblock.com or call 1-800-624-2120, ext. 800.

PITTSBURGH CORNING GLASS BLOCK®

Made in the USA.

STYLISH, SAFE, AND MAINTENANCE FREE.
AND TO THINK,
THE PRICE MAY BE ITS MOST ATTRACTIVE FEATURE.

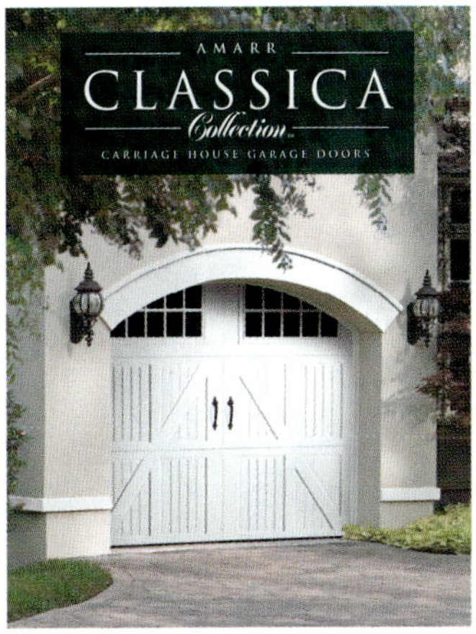

The garage door. It may be the largest, single variable in establishing the look of a home. Nothing creates a more stylish compliment to a home than a carriage house door from our Classica Collection. Classic carriage house design. Pinch-resistant DuraSafe technology. Maintenance free all-steel construction. Surprising affordability. Classica, the timeless design that will stand the test of time.

Amarr® GARAGE DOORS

THE CLASSICA COLLECTION DOORS ARE AVAILABLE IN FOUR BASE DESIGNS AND EIGHT TOP SECTIONS PROVIDING A CHOICE OF 32 DIFFERENT DESIGN OPTIONS.

LUCERN

VALENCIA

SANTIAGO

TUSCANY

PINCH-RESISTANT DuraSafe System SAFE & DURABLE™

FOR MORE INFORMATION ON THE BEAUTIFUL AND AFFORDABLE CLASSICA COLLECTION CARRIAGE HOUSE DOORS FROM AMARR, CALL 800.503.DOOR. OR VISIT US AT WWW.AMARR.COM

The Weslock Way.

CYLINDRICAL DESIGN • PUSH BUTTON LOCKING • CONCEALED SCREWS

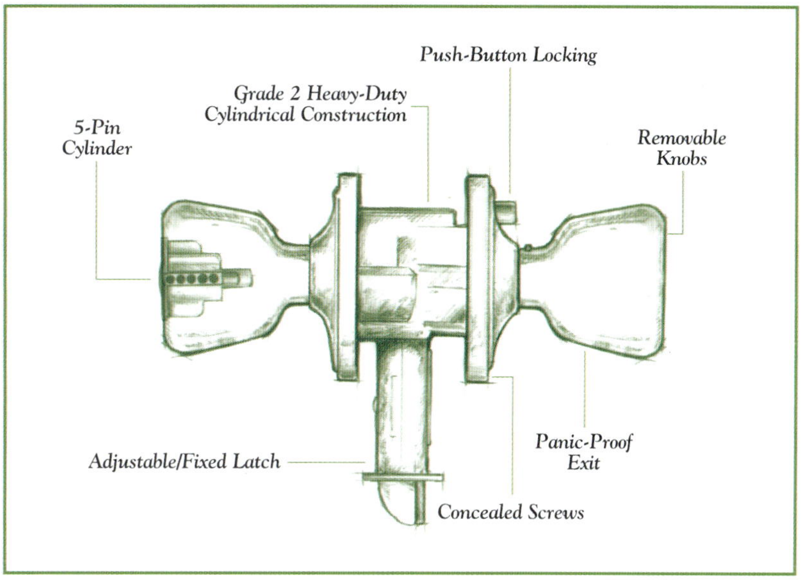

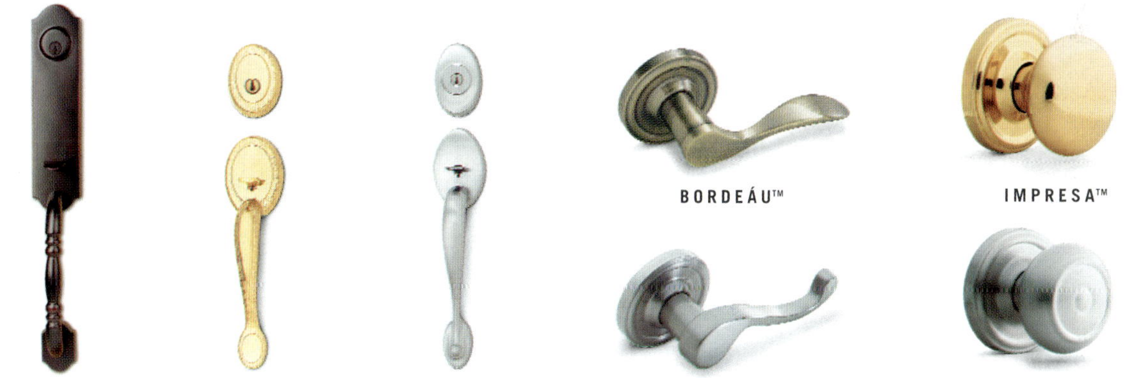

MANSION™ OVAL™ LEXINGTON™ BORDEÁU™ CALAIS™ IMPRESA™ SAVANNAH™

SECURITY, SAFETY & STYLE

WESLOCK products represent the highest standards when it comes to **SECURITY, SAFETY & STYLE.** With Weslock, you ***can*** have it all.

Weslock is proud to provide your home with added security by offering the only **residential Grade II cylindrical locksets** in the industry. As well, each lockset comes equipped with our **exclusive push-button safety feature,** making our locks panic-proof & preventing lockouts. And finally, Weslock always keeps your home's unique decor in mind by offering a **wide variety of styles & finishes**. With Weslock products, you'll never have to sacrifice security & safety for style again.

Call 800.575.2658 to learn more about our Nelson Design Group promotion!

Weslock®

www.weslock.com PHONE 800.575.2658 FAX 918.294.3869

NDG Corporate Partner - SmartChoice Product

IWP® Aurora™ composite doors from JELD-WEN just won't grow old. While we design doors with the visual intrigue of old-world, weathered wood doors, each one will consistently perform like it was installed just yesterday. In fact, IWP Aurora doors are engineered to withstand harsh weather and extreme temperatures for years. These benefits, as well as a host of designs and options, are sure to attract your customers. To learn more about reliable JELD-WEN® doors, visit **www.jeld-wen.com/auroradoors.**
Shown: IWP Aurora AU201322; Inset, IWP Aurora Knotty Alder AU201322.

RELIABILITY *for* real life™

JELD-WEN® WINDOWS & DOORS

Problem
Solution
AuraLast
Solid pine AuraLast,™
THE WORRY-FREE WOOD
from JELD-WEN
Superior protection from wood decay
Superior protection from water absorption
Superior protection from termite infestation
Backed by an industry-leading 20-year warranty

Why an L.J. Smith Stair System is the best choice...

It's important to us that your stairway is not only functional and beautiful, but that it safely carries you and your loved ones from one floor to another for decades to come. L.J. Smith's stairway components are uniquely designed so they provide the strongest, most durable and attractive stairway, when installed properly. You will have peace of mind knowing you made the right choice with the stair components manufacturer who is recognized as the leader and innovator in the industry for over one hundred years...L.J. Smith.

Custom pre-built straight, circular and spiral stairways are also available from Woodsmiths Design and Manufacturing, a division of L.J. Smith. Woodsmiths uses only genuine L.J. Smith stair parts in their wood stairs, however, their abilities also include carved wood turnings, glass, metals and even molded plastics.

For more information on L.J. Smith products, visit www.ljsmith.net, contact your local lumber dealer or call us at (740) 269-2221.

For more information on Woodsmiths Design & Manufacturing capabilities, visit www.woodsmiths.net or call us at (800) 874-2876.

Instant sales appeal. Lasting allergy relief.

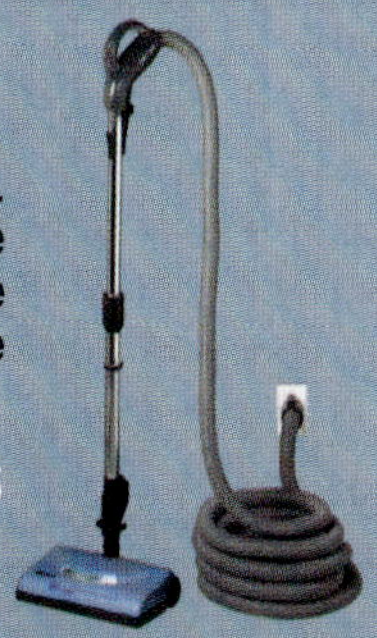

©Copyright 2004 Coastal Living/John O'Hagan

INNOVATION The new Dave Lennox Signature™ Integrated Comfort Solution delivers the ultimate in all areas important to your customers — comfort, control, efficiency, quiet operation, reliability, indoor air quality and environmental responsibility. The components can be installed separately or, for maximum effectiveness, integrated together. They provide better efficiency not only as individual products, but also as a system solution. Plus the air conditioners and furnaces are the quietest on the market today. And with non-ozone-depleting refrigerants, they are more environmentally friendly.

CONTROL The entire system is tied together and controlled with the Lennox SignatureStat™ Home Comfort Controller. It gives homeowners the ability to establish both humidity and temperature setpoints from one central location. The Harmony III Zoning system allows the customer to have consistent airflow throughout the home, providing even temperatures whether the system is heating or cooling. This allows the customer to customize their comfort based on need.

COMFORT Indoor air quality is a major part of comfort and a growing concern for many homeowners. Our PureAir™ home air purifier can clean indoor air better than any other single system. It's the only indoor air quality system to attack all three classes of indoor air contaminants — particles, bioaerosols and odors/chemicals. It removes irritating particles and bioaerosols from the airstream with an effective MERV 9 filter. And our patented photocatalytic technology removes odors and chemicals, leaving the home's air pure.

RELIABILITY Our integrated system offers solutions to household challenges as well. Our unique System Operations Monitor tells homeowners via a light on the SignatureStat thermostat if there is a problem with the condensing unit or heat pump. Such easy detection of problems creates peace of mind for the customer and helps technicians with troubleshooting. That's good news for everyone.

At Lennox we're proud to continue our heritage of innovation and reliability by helping you offer easy and complete solutions for the home comfort needs of your customers.

DAVE LENNOX signature™ COLLECTION

We Encourage Professionalism Through Technician Certification by NATE

ENERGY STAR Partner of the Year

LENNOX®
A BETTER PLACE

To learn more about our heating, cooling, air quality and fireplace products, visit lennox.com or call 1-800-4-LENNOX.

www.lennox.com AOL Keyword: LENNOX 1-800-4-LENNOX

ORGANIZE WITH REV-A-SHELF®

We have hundreds of storage organizers to fit your cabinet needs!

Polymer and White Wire Accessories

Wood Classic Accessories

Premiere Accessories

Rev-A-Shelf is renowned as the industry's leading cabinet organization manufacturer with an extensive selection of products designed to increase space in cabinets throughout the home and office. Order our new and improved full-color catalog today to browse through the hundreds of storage solutions for the kitchen, closet, vanity, and more.

Rev-A-Shelf. We are going to change the way you think about cabinet organization!

Visit us at rev-a-shelf.com/nelson for a list of Rev-A-Shelf dealers and distributors in your area.

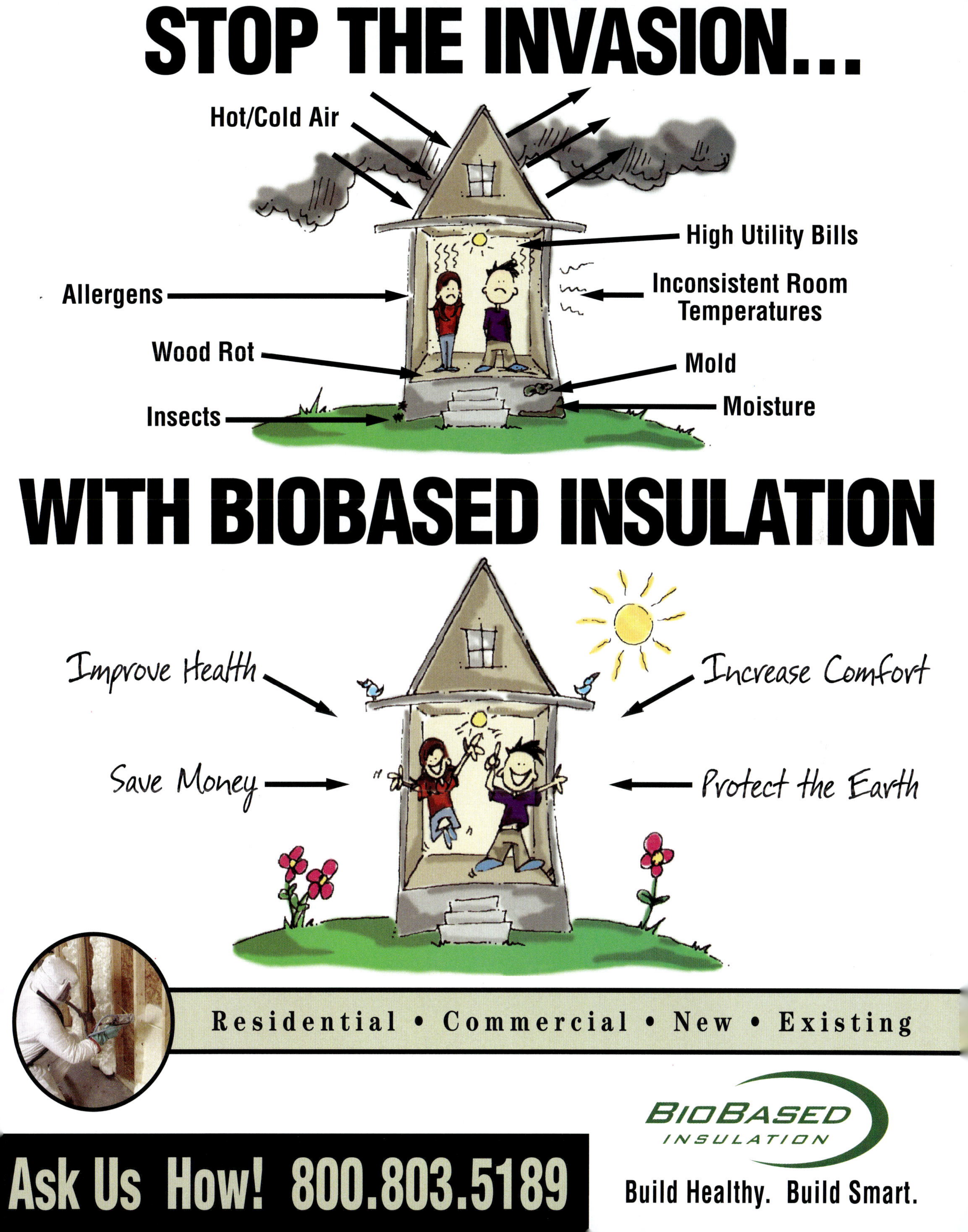
STOP THE INVASION...
Hot/Cold Air
High Utility Bills
Allergens
Inconsistent Room Temperatures
Wood Rot
Mold
Insects
Moisture
WITH BIOBASED INSULATION
Improve Health
Increase Comfort
Save Money
Protect the Earth
Residential • Commercial • New • Existing
BIOBASED INSULATION
Ask Us How! 800.803.5189
Build Healthy. Build Smart.

Fashion comes in many forms, which is why Hanson Brick offers hundreds of colors and textures to turn the house you design into a home. To learn more about our latest line, call 877-HANSON8 or visit us at www.hansonbrick.com.
Hanson
The face of brick™
What the best-dressed homes wear.

84® HOMES

84lumber.com

WHO WE ARE

84 Lumber Company is the largest privately held supplier of building materials in the United States. Founded in 1956 by Joe Hardy in the town of Eighty Four, Pennsylvania, 20 miles south of Pittsburgh, 84 Lumber is still growing. In 2005, we'll open 50 new stores, raising the company's store count to over 500 locations in 34 states coast-to-coast. In two of the past three years,84 Lumber sold more building materials to professional contractors and remodelers than any other supplier, with 2004 sales exceeding $3.3 billion.

OUR MISSION

84 Lumber Company is dedicated to being the low cost provider of lumber and building materials to professional builders,remodelers and dedicated do-it-yourselfers, while adding value to our quality products through a trained, knowledgeable andmotivated team of professional sales associates.

WHAT WE OFFER

- Competitive Prices
- Top Quality Products
- Knowledgeable Associates
- Special Order Program
- Convenient Hours
- Professional Delivery

FINANCING OPTIONS

84 Lumber provides many fast, builder-friendly financing options with our same down-to-earth value and convenience.

INVENTORY & VOLUME BUYING POWER

With over 500 stores and a centralized buying system, customers can take advantage of our national purchasing power to save money and add more to their bottom line. Through our established relationships with national suppliers and bulk buying power, you can rely on 84 to have the products and quantities you need.

- Lumber
- Plywood
- Insulation
- Trim
- Mouldings
- Flooring
- Siding
- Drywall
- Decks
- Trusses
- Roofing
- Skylights
- Engineered Lumber
- Hardware
- Doors and Windows
- Kitchens and Baths
- Storage Buildings
- 84 Home Packages

MEETING THE NEEDS OF PROFESSIONAL BUILDERS

To meet the special needs of the professional builder, 84 Lumber has assembled a well-trained contractor sales force of more than 1,200 associates nationwide, with each of the company's stores having two to four contractor sales representatives (CSR's) on staff. Each new CSR goes through an extensive training and development program, and attends on-going courses throughout their career to stay current on the latest building trends and new services available. Our CSR's truly understand that every contractor has their own unique set of needs relating to service, product selection, delivery, and financing, just to name a few. Our CSR's strive to learn the operation of each contractor's business so that 84 Lumber may serve you as efficiently as possible.

SPECIAL ORDER PROGRAM & BUILDING COMPONENTS

While our stores are well stocked with many basic building materials, we also have an outstanding special order program which allows virtually any custom product to be ordered through any 84 Lumber store associate or CSR. We will cater to a wide range of tastes by ordering those hard-to-find products, to be delivered when you need them, in most cases, directly to a job site if requested. 84 Lumber also operates building component manufacturing facilities in major markets, producing roof and floor trusses, as well as wall panels to help builders become more efficient and profitable.

COMPUTERIZED BIDS AND PRICING

Give us your materials list, blueprints, sketches or ideas and we will process your estimate within 24 hours and your blueprint take-off within 48 hours. If you're not ready to start your next project now, 84 offers a 30-day price guarantee. Pay for the materials now to lock in current prices, and you'll have up to 30 days to pick up your materials without any change in cost to you!

FAST AND RELIABLE DELIVERY

We know your time is important, and we won't waste it. Careful scheduling assures that materials are delivered to the job site when you need them. If you prefer, our convenient "drive up and load" sheds with express loading allow you to spend more time on your project and less time pulling carts through those crowded "superstores".

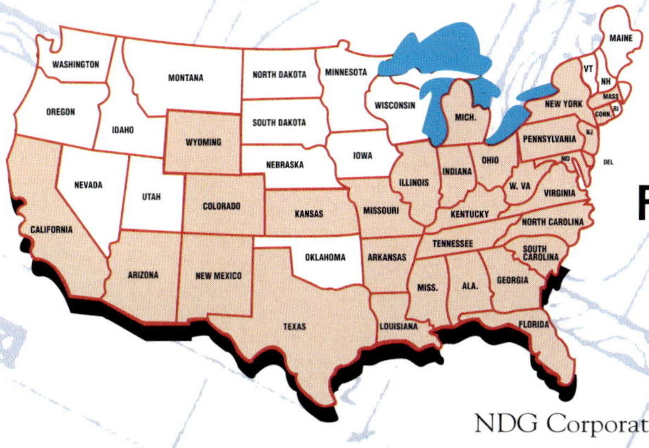

For the 84 Lumber location nearest you call:

1-800-359-8484